APOCALYPSE

The People's Bible

Apocalypse

The Gospel according to St. John
The Letters of St. John
The Revelation of St. John

newly translated by Rabbi Sidney Brichto

Sinclair-Stevenson

First published in Great Britain by
Sinclair-Stevenson
3 South Terrace, London SW7 2TB

British Library Cataloguing in Publication Data
A CIP catalogue record for this book is available from the British Library.

ISBN 0 9540476 9 9

Typeset by Rowland Phototypesetting Ltd, Bury St Edmunds, Suffolk
Printed and bound by Bookmarque Ltd, Croydon, Surrey

Contents

Preface

When I set out on the project of making the Bible more accessible to ordinary readers, my intention was not to retranslate it but to cast an existing readable translation into a user-friendly format. When that turned out not be be possible, I undertook a new translation. Many were surprised that a rabbi should translate the New Testament, but I had no alternative, if my mission was to win for the Bible readers whose interest was based not on the search for faith but on an appreciation of the skills, oratorical and literary, which made it the most revered library of books in the West. As a translator, I would need to put my value judgements aside and treat the writings of a competitive faith with as much objectivity as my own religious and literary heritage.

I am very glad both that an existing translation was not available for my purpose and that I did not flinch from coming to grips with the Christian Bible, in spite of the fact that it had been used to fan the hatred of Jews into a fever pitch which cost countless innocent lives. I have learnt so much, because in the act of translating I was compelled to read every sentence carefully and without pre-judgements. I found that the text told me more by this method than by the consultation of renowned biblical scholars. This was especially the case with the *Gospel according to John*. Too often, scholars begin with prejudices due to their faith and commitment or to the joy of writing books to contradict their colleagues. The fact is that the texts speak for themselves if we let them. They do, however, require knowledge of the countervailing tensions when they were written.

While the New Testament was taboo in an orthodox Jewish home, I learned in my state school to love the story of Jesus and his parables from the gospels of *Matthew, Mark* and *Luke. John* and *Revelation* were not read because they were too difficult. For this reason, in explaining what I believe to be the clear meaning of these texts, I have had to provide voluminous footnotes. As referring to the footnotes can mar your enjoyment, do it only when you feel the need. Alternatively, first read the footnotes as a student, then read the texts again as a good read with the added pleasure which comes from increased understanding.

The *Gospel according to John*, the *Letters of John* and *Revelation* make a good unit, as they come from the same pen, or if not that, at least from the same school of style and thought. My reasons for having this view will be revealed in the introductions to these books.

N.B.
Words or sentences set in **bold font** are editorial additions.

The Gospel according to St John

Introduction

The Fourth Gospel is a remarkable literary feat. The power of its poetic statement of the Christian faith continues to hold its believers in thrall, in spite of all the worldly evidence against it. Indeed, St. John, through his eloquence, raises the world of the spirit to a level, which makes materialists ashamed of their narrow vision of happiness. In the hands of St. John, the life of Jesus is given the same cosmic significance as the creation of the world. His history is an epic, and so like my treatment of *Genesis* needs to be translated as such.

What is enchanting about this gospel is that the humanity of Jesus is as beautifully portrayed, as is his divinity.[1] Jesus as man is made to speak like a god living on earth. No heroic tale is more sensual than that of Mary massaging Jesus's feet with the most expensive oil and then wiping them with her hair; and the irony of his defence of her to his disciples for not distributing the value of the oil to the poor; "The poor will always be with you, but you will not always have me." Were his disciples suffering from envy at seeing the worship he inspired in a woman? But then, on the night of his arrest Jesus undresses, except for a towel, wrapped around his waist. He washes his disciples feet and dries them with the towel which was covering his nakedness. Jesus, the man-god can become the servant of men as well as the idol of women.

The literary deftness and humour of St. John is revealed in the dialogue of the blind man healed by Jesus and the leaders who wish to condemn him for his cure. The blind beggar mocks their authority by the superiority of his own logic and wit, and we, the readers, rejoice in his moral victory over them.

The story of the adulterous woman brought to Jesus for condemnation could not be improved. The scribes quote to him the

---

[1] I am, of course writing this from the perspective of those who believe that he was both.

Law of Moses, which ordains death for the adulterer. He looks to the ground where he is moving his pointing finger in the dust. Without raising his head, he avoids the question, "He of you who is sinless, let him cast the first stone." One by one, they all drift away, until when he stands up, the woman who could have walked away, is the only one there. He sends her off with the words, "Sin no more."

The images are very visual. One feels the closeness between Jesus and the disciple he loves most. He is described as snuggling by his side during the last supper. The jealousy that Peter has for him is not hidden, as Jesus reprimands him. All that Jesus does, he does for effect; and why not, for that, according to the narrator, is his purpose in coming down to earth: in becoming flesh to redeem humanity from the imprisonment of the flesh.

St. John, unlike the other gospels is written in a crisp, clear and sequential fashion. Jesus explains his behaviour to his disciples. He leaves nothing in doubt. The reason for many of the footnotes is to explain the theological development of Christianity as revealed by St. John. I hope these will give a greater appreciation of the content of the message without diminishing the mysterious beauty of its form.

*   *   *

St. John is the culmination of New Testament theology. The debate on Jesus's identity is concluded! Throughout the gospels, the identity of Jesus is debated. Who is he: a prophet, the Messiah-King who was crucified but resurrected to restore the sovereignty of Israel, the Son of God who was sacrificed to redeem all humanity from sin and death? All the options are argued in *St. John*, but the decision is conclusive: Jesus is man because he is born from a woman; he is divine because God was his father. Furthermore, the purpose of his resurrection was not to remove the yoke of Roman oppression and restore himself as the head of the Davidic House, but to be his father's sacrifice to usher in the Kingdom of God.

Biblical scholars write about the Johannine School among the early Christians. I find this nomenclature difficult to justify, for it appears to me that St. John says nothing that St. Paul did not previously teach. In fact, he is putting into the mouth of Jesus the theology of Paul.

It might be too difficult for a believing Christian to accept that it was not the apostles, witnessing the life and death of Jesus and taught by him after his resurrection, who instituted the new covenant, but that it was St. Paul, who never met Jesus except in a vision, who founded Christianity. The truth of this problem was revealed to me on informing a nun that it was apparent that the Comforter, who Jesus predicts to his disciples will come after his death to explain all his teachings, could be none other than St. Paul. She vehemently denied the possibility, not on the basis of the evidence, but because, as she exclaimed: "That would make Paul more important than Jesus!" A Cardinal who served in the Vatican to whom I submitted the idea was less dismissive, "Why should it not be Paul?"

The discomfort in giving St. Paul such status is increased at the observation that his rival, St. Peter, while never being denied as the chief disciple is not his master's favourite. There must also be some significance in the fact that while the four gospels differ on many points, they agree that Peter was to deny Jesus three times before his crucifixion. The moving scene at the cross, after the clothes of Jesus are divided among the soldiers, not only reveals his love for his mother and his special disciple, but St. Peter's absence. Should he not have been there to implore his forgiveness and to show his loyalty? Perhaps he was there, but none of the gospels deigned to report it. My reading of it: Peter was a powerful fisherman, firm in his faith that Jesus was the Messiah who had come to throw off the Roman yoke and become the king of the Jews. He carries a sword to fight the Romans to make Jesus king. He cuts off the right ear of the High Priest's servant to prevent Jesus's arrest. His denial of his relationship to Jesus is due to the knowledge that the game is up: the rebellion is not to take place, and he, as an accomplice, is in danger. After his death, he believes that at the appointed time, Jesus will return to complete his work, indicated in the beginning of *Acts*, which is the messianic redemption of the Jews, but *not* to appear on the right hand of God on Judgement Day when, according to *St. Matthew* and *St. Luke*, the apostles will be seated on thrones alongside their lord, the Son of God.

As a Jew who cannot be expected to accept the Christian faith, it is not heretical for me to maintain the view that the disciples, coming out of their Jewish background, could not have believed that Jesus was the Son of God destined to die as a sacrificial atonement for humanity. The very fact that Pontius Pilate, informed by Jesus that his kingdom is not of this world, still hauls him before the Jews and says 'Here is your king!' is proof that he is not being crucified for his heretical claim of divine status, even though the text gives this as one of the reasons. More realistic, though equally fanciful, is the Jews' accusation against Pilate: "If you release this man, you are no friend of Caesar's for anyone who claims to be king rebels against Caesar." And earlier, (and this is feasible) the High Priest Caiaphas recommends the surrender of Jesus to the Romans because the acceptance of Jesus as the Messiah-king would give them an excuse to destroy the Jewish people.

The transfiguration of Jesus from the son of man, the Messiah-King to the Son of God, Christ, is foreshadowed in Acts where Christian history moves on from Peter to Paul. Peter will only be mentioned in connection with the mandate he gives to Paul to become the apostle to the Gentiles and confirmation that a convert to Christ need not take on the religious obligations of the Jews. Forgive me if I suggest that Peter only reluctantly agreed to this, nor did he, as recorded in *Acts*, have a vision in which he is told to eat forbidden meat. Were this so, there would have been no record in his letters of Paul calling Peter a hypocrite for refusing to eat with the Gentiles. We must never forget that Paul's letters are our first record of Christian doctrine; the gospels and the *Acts of the Apostles* were written later and are subject to the need to give a mission statement to believers and a uniform message to potential converts. The New Testament, in spite of its contradictions, arrives at Paul's doctrine, which is powerfully and poetically formulated in *St. John*.

If one wonders why the claim of Jesus's messianic identity was not altogether removed from the text, the answer is that it could not be, because to survive in the Roman Empire, Christianity required a biblical basis so as to make it part of Judaism. Judaism was respected by Rome as a religion of great antiquity; Rome despised new religions as wild and fanatic: *superstitio*. Christianity needed Jewish respectability to escape further persecution. It is significant that the very term, Christian, was first used in Antioch, a Gentile city, where Paul taught for a year; the term had not been used in Judea.

One aspect of Pauline theology which is reinforced by the Fourth Gospel is the extent to which Christian life is seen as a prelude and preparation for the End of Days. The Kingdom of God is not to be realised in this material world. The Second Coming will not be the return of Jesus to rule this world; it will be to return to usher believers into the heavenly world, when sinners will be utterly condemned. Jesus comforts his disciples on his death:

> "After I go to prepare a place for you,
> I will return and take you to myself;
> That where I am you will be . . ."

Jesus will come not to live among them but to bring them to God, so that they may live in his presence. The painful message is that faith and goodness cannot be triumphant on earth, but only in the hereafter. When his followers question Paul over the delay in the return of Jesus, reminding him that since his promise, many believers in Christ have died, he reassures them that when the great day comes, the faithful dead will come down from heaven and the faithful living will rise and meet them in mid-air. It is a hard message to live by, but perhaps no more difficult for believers in the Jewish faith who wait for salvation in this world which never seems to come. The apocalyptic dimension of Christian faith finds its visionary expression in *Revelation's* grand vision of the creation of a New Jerusalem descending from heaven to earth.

*   *   *

The *Letters of John* require no special introduction, as I take the traditional view that they were written by the gospel's author, or at least were inspired by him, as they reflect his faith and genius for communicating it to others.

THE GOSPEL ACCORDING TO ST. JOHN

1 John's prologue

In the beginning was the Word[1] and
The Word was with God[2] and
The Word was God.[3]
He[4] was with God at the very beginning.
All things were created through him;
Without him nothing created would have come into being.
He was the source of life –
The life that was the light[5] of mankind.
The light still shines in the darkness
And the darkness cannot extinguish it.

A man was sent by God,
His name was John, **the Baptiser**.
This man came to give witness to the Light,
So that, through him, all would become believers.
He was not the Light but a witness to the Light –
The true Light that enlightens everyone,
Who was about to come into the world.

He was, **of course,** already in the world[6] –
For through him was the world created –[7]

---

[1] The Word of God, which created the world, is personified. The fact that the creation story in *Genesis* starts with the same words: 'In the beginning' is not a coincidence but intended to reinforce that Christ was there when the world came into being.

[2] The Word is contiguous with God.

[3] The Word is identified with God.

[4] Jesus is the word of God

[5] Light is the symbol of the life of the spirit.

[6] As part of the godhead, Jesus was already in the world, but not as God become man.

[7] As God created the world through the word, i.e., "And the Lord said: 'Let there be light and there was light,'" Christ, as the 'Word' was the vehicle for the creation of the world. In Jewish tradition, the Torah was the vehicle.

But the world did not know him.
He came to his own people who would not accept him.[1]
But to those who received him
He gave the power to become the children of God.
Those who believed in his name
No longer were born, **as though,** through flesh and blood,
Nor through the lust of the flesh or human purpose;
They were now born of God.[2]

So the Word became flesh and lived among us.
We saw his glory, the glory seemly to a father's only son –
Overflowing with grace and truth.
John testified concerning him as he cried out,
"This is He of whom I said: 'He who comes after me
Supersedes me because he in fact preceded me.'"
From his fullness we have received
One gracious gift in place of another:
The Law was given through Moses,
Grace and truth came through Jesus Christ.[3]
No man has seen God, but he has revealed
His only son who rests in the bosom of his father.[4]

The testimony of John the Baptiser

This was John's testimony when the Jews of Jerusalem sent
Priests and Levites to ask him: "Who are you?"[5]
He replied with unqualified candour, "I am not the Messiah."

---

[1] This is not altogether true, as the apostles were Jewish – an indication that, by the time this was written, the Jewish-Christian sect had disappeared.
[2] By believing in Jesus, they, like him, become children of God and are re-born to eternal life.
[3] Christ is the derivative of Greek *christus* meaning *anointed one*, i.e., king. In my translation of the synoptic gospels, *christus* was translated as *the anointed one*; as *John* is a theological gospel in which Jesus is recognised as the Son of God and saviour, I use the appellative Christ which reflects the divinity assigned to him.
[4] There are variant readings in the original Greek texts of the last two lines. While this alters the translations, the meaning remains very much the same.
[5] Was he the Messiah?

– "Who are you then, are you Elijah?"[1]
– "No I am not."
– "Are you the prophet?"[2]
– "No."
– "Who are you then?
    What answer can we give to those who sent us?
    How would you describe yourself?"
– "I am the one, of whom Isaiah the prophet spoke – **I am**
    The voice crying in the wilderness,
    'Clear the way for the LORD.' "[3]

The Pharisees among them questioned him,
"By whose authority do you baptise,
"If you are not the Messiah nor Elijah nor the Prophet?"
– "I baptise in water; **I only call the people to repent,**
    In your midst stands one, whom you acknowledge not –
    The one who will supersede me,
    The laces of whose sandals I am unworthy to tie."
[These events took place in Bethany,[4]
On the other side of the Jordan,
Where John was baptising.]

---

[1] Malachi, the last of the prophets, prophesies, "See, I am sending you Elijah the prophet before the coming of the day of the LORD – great and awesome! [3:23] Earlier he declares, "See, I am sending my messenger; he shall clear the path before me." [3:1] The fact that Elijah was scooped up by God in a whirlwind is the basis for the Jewish belief that he will reappear to announce the coming of the Messiah.

[2] Moses *(Deuteronomy 18:15)* says that God will raise up a prophet like himself. Is this John or Jesus? Later, in the text, the crowds wonder whether Jesus is the pre-ordained prophet.

[3] Isaiah 40:3

[4] This is not the famous Bethany, some two miles from Jerusalem on the eastern slope of the Mount of Olives.

The encounter of John the baptiser with Jesus

The next day, John saw Jesus coming towards him.
He declared, "Look, the Lamb of God[1]
Who takes away the sin of the world;
This is he of whom I said: after me comes a man
Who supersedes me because he in fact came before me.
I did not know the form he was to take.
Yet, to hasten the time for his revelation to Israel,
I baptised **sinners** in water."

Then John gave this testimony:
"I saw the **Divine** Spirit come like a dove from heaven.
He rested on him, but I did not know who he was,
But He who sent me[2] to baptise in water –
He said to me, "On whomever you see
The spirit descending and resting
That is he who will baptise with the Divine Spirit.[3]
This I have seen and testify: he is the chosen one of God."

The next day, John was there with two of his disciples.
Seeing Jesus walking by, he cried, "Look, the Lamb of God."
When they heard him say this, they followed Jesus.
Turning around, he saw them following him:
"What do you want?"
– "Rabbi (which means teacher), where are you staying?"
– "Come and see."
So they went and saw where he was staying;
They remained with him that day.
It was at the tenth hour.[4]

---

[1] While *Acts 8:32* compares Jesus to 'a dumb lamb going to the slaughter', it is only here and in *Revelation* that Jesus is visualised as the Lamb of God.
[2] Who else could this be but God? Why does he not say so? Is John acknowledging a divine inspiration whose source he cannot identify?
[3] In *Acts 19*, Paul distinguishes between the baptism of John which is to achieve repentance and that of Jesus which grants the grace of the divine spirit.
[4] About 4pm.

Andrew (Simon Peter's brother), one of the two disciples
Who had followed him, immediately went to his brother
  Simon:
"We have found the Messiah (which means Christ)."
He led him to Jesus, who looked at him:
"You are Simon the son of John,
You will be called Cephas (which means Peter)."[1]
The next day, wishing to go to the Galilee,
Jesus found Philip;[2] he said to him, "Follow me."
Now, Philip had come from Bethsaida –
The town of Andrew and Simon Peter.
Philip went and told Nathaniel:
"We have found the one whom Moses wrote about in the Law,
And about whom the prophets also wrote –
Jesus the son of Joseph of Nazareth." Nathaniel protested,
"Nazareth? Can any thing good come from there?"
– "Come and see."
When Jesus saw Nathaniel approaching, he exclaimed,
"Here is a worthy Israelite in whom there is no deceit."
– "How do you know me?"
– "Before Philip found you, I saw you under the fig tree."
– "Rabbi, you are the Son of God; you are the king of Israel!"
– "Do you then believe because I told you that
  I saw you under the fig tree?
  You shall see greater things then that:
  In truth I tell you, you shall all see the heavens open,
  And angels ascending and descending on the Son of Man."[3]

---

[1] Both *cephas* (Aramaic) and *peter* (Greek) mean *rock*.

[2] In the other three Gospels, we know nothing of Philip excepting that he is listed among the Twelve Apostles.

[3] The image is that of the LORD's Messengers going up and down a ladder in Jacob's vision at Beth-el.

2 The wedding at Cana

Two days later, a wedding took place in Cana in Galilee.
As Jesus's mother was to be there,
He and his disciples were invited.
When there was no more wine, Jesus's mother said to him:
"They have not provided enough wine."
– "Woman, of what concern is this to me or to you?
  My hour has not yet come."[1]
All the same, his mother instructed the servants,
"Do whatever he tells you." Nearby were six stone water jars
Which Jews used for ritual purification,
Each holding between twenty and thirty gallons.
Jesus says to them, "Fill the jars with water."
They filled them to the brim; then Jesus says,
"Now draw some off and take it to the steward."
They did so; when the steward tasted it –
The water becoming wine, he did not know its source.
(Only the servants who drew the water knew.)
The steward took the bridegroom aside and complimented him,
"People serve the best wine first;
And when the guests are drunk the worst,
But you have saved the best for now."
This was the first of the signs Jesus did in Galilee,
To reveal his glory; and his disciples believed in him.

Jesus drives out the money-changers

Then he went down to Capernaum with his mother,
Brothers and disciples where he stayed for a few days.
As the Jewish Passover drew near, he went to Jerusalem.
In the Temple Court, he saw men selling oxen, sheep and doves
And moneychangers sitting behind tables.[2]

---

[1] To reveal his divine power to perform miracles.
[2] This was to be expected as they were buying and selling animals for the sacrifices in different coinage.

Making a whip from rope, he drove them out of the Temple-
The sheep and the oxen; he overturned the tables of the
Moneychangers and scattered all their coins.
To those who were selling doves, he said,
"Take these things out of here.
Do not make my father's house into a market-place!"
His disciples then remembered what was written,
"Zeal for your house has consumed me."[1]

The Jews then demanded of him,
"What sign can you give us which entitles you to do this?"[2]
– "Destroy this shrine; I will raise it again in three days."
– "What! It took forty-six years to build this shrine,
   And you will raise it again in three days?"
Ah, but he was speaking of the shrine which was his body,
Once he was raised from the dead,
His disciples remembered what he had said.
Then they believed the Scriptures and the words of Jesus.

Now, while he was in Jerusalem during the Passover festival,
Many, witnessing the signs he was performing, believed in him.
But Jesus had no confidence in them because
He knew the nature of men.
He had no need for their evidence about any man
For he understood the character of men.[3]

3 Jesus promises eternal life to who those who believe

Now, a Pharisee, Nicodemus, a Jewish leader,
Came to Jesus by night:
"Rabbi, we know that you are a teacher sent by God;
For no one could perform such signs as these

[1] *Psalms 69:10.*
[2] In other words, "Let's have a miracle to prove your authority."
[3] He knew that faith built on miracles would not last.

Unless God was with him."
– "In truth I tell you, unless a man is born again,
  He cannot see the Kingdom of God."
– "How can a man be born when he is old; can he enter
  His mother's womb a second time to be born?"
– "In truth I tell you – a man not born of water and Spirit[1]
  Cannot enter the Kingdom of God.
  Flesh is born of flesh; but Spirit is born of Spirit.
  Do not be shocked when I said that you must be born again:
  The wind blows where it wills; you hear its sound,
  But you do not know its source or direction.
  So it is with everyone who is born of the Spirit."
– "How does this come about?"
– "You, a teacher of Israel, do not know?
  In truth I tell you, we speak about what we know,
  And we bear witness to what we have seen,
  But you do not accept our testimony.
  If you do not believe me when I speak of earthly matters,[2]
  How will you believe me when I talk of heavenly things?

"Now no man has gone up to heaven, except the one
Who came down from heaven – the Son of Man;[3]
Now just as Moses lifted up the snake in the wilderness,[4]

---

[1] Those bathed in God's spirit through baptism and faith.

[2] The earthly matters are the miracles that Jesus has performed

[3] This is a clear reference to *Daniel* 7:13–14: 'In a vision of the night, I saw what looked like a son of man riding the heavenly clouds. He went towards the Ancient of Ages (God) and was brought close to him. He was granted dominion, glory and a kingdom, that all peoples, nations and languages should obey him. His ruling power is everlasting, which shall not pass away and his kingdom will never be destroyed.' This was the promised Messiah from the House of David. One can only speculate whether already by the time that *Daniel* was written, the scion of David had been transformed from ordinary flesh and blood into a divine figure. I think that before Jesus was deemed to be a divine being, 'the son of man' was a figure of speech for a human being.

[4] Among other signs Moses turned his staff into a snake to persuade Pharoah of his divine mission. Jesus will need to be lifted up to heaven to persuade the world to believe in him. Alternatively, this could refer to the bronze serpent

By which sign, he was believed to come from God,
So must the Son of Man be lifted up by **God into heaven,**
So that all who believe in him may attain eternal life.[1]
For God so loved the world that he gave his
One and only son,[2] so that everyone who believed in him
Would not perish but have life eternal.
God did not send his son into the world to judge the world,
But that the world might be saved through him.
He who believes in him will not be judged;
He who does not believe in him has already been judged
Because he has not believed
In the name of God's one and only son.

"But men preferred darkness to light
Because of their wicked behaviour.
All who act wickedly hate the light
And will not come into the light in the fear that
They will be condemned for their wicked deeds.
But whoever lives by the truth comes into the light
To prove that what he has done is because of God."[3]

The baptisms of Jesus cause concern John reassures his disciple

After this, Jesus and his disciples went into Judea.
He stayed with them and performed baptisms.
John was also baptising[4] in Ainon, near Salim

---

which Moses raised onto a standard. The Israelites who had been bitten as
punishment by flying serpents would live if they looked at it.
[1] According to the narrative, Jesus is now projecting into the divine drama of
his crucifixion and resurrection. As it is hardly likely that Jesus himself would
have taught the profound mystery of Christian dogma, which follows, I treat it
as John's soliloquy.
[2] On reading these words, it is difficult not to think of the story of Abraham's
near-sacrifice of Isaac. (*Genesis 22:1*)
[3] This observation is discouraging for repentant sinners in which the synoptic
gospels abound.
[4] Nowhere else are we told that Jesus baptised and John were baptising at the
same time. Having declared that he was only preparing the way for Jesus, one

Because of the abundance of water there.
(This was before John was put into prison.)
There occurred a dispute between John's disciples
And a Jew over the matter of purification.
They came to John and said to him,
"Rabbi, that man who was with you beyond the Jordan –
The one to whom you bore witness –
Look – this man is now baptising
And everyone is flocking to him."
– "Can a man receive but what comes from heaven?
You, yourselves, heard me say that I was not the Messiah,
But he who was sent ahead of him.
The bride [the disciples] belongs to the bridegroom.
But, the friend who is in attendance on the bridegroom
Who stands by him and listens rejoices when he hears
The bridegroom's voice. This joy is mine; it is now fulfilled.
He must grow in greatness while mine decreases.

"The one who comes from above [heaven] is above all;
The one from earth, being of earth, speaks of earthly things.
The one who comes from heaven is above all.
He gives witness to what he has seen and heard,
Yet no one accepts his testimony.
Those accepting his testimony confirm God's truth.
The one sent by God speaks God's words;
He has been given of his spirit without any limit.
The Father loves the Son; he has given all into his hand.
The one who believes in the Son gains life eternal;
But he who denies the Son will not behold life eternal,
But the wrath of God will be upon him."

---

would have thought that John the Baptiser would have become one of his disciples. The fact that he did not could make one think that the accreditation of Jesus by John the Baptiser happened after the event to exploit his popularity in the Jewish imagination to reinforce the claims of the apostles on behalf of their master.

4 Jesus and the Samaritan woman
He explains his mission to the disciples

When the Lord heard what the Pharisees were saying –
That Jesus was gaining and baptising more disciples than John,
(Though it was not Jesus, but his disciples, who baptised)[1]
He left Judea to return again to Galilee.
Needing to pass through Samaria, he arrived at Sychar,
A town in Samaria near the plot of land Jacob had given to his
    son Joseph;
As Jacob's well was there, Jesus, weary from his journey,
Sat down by the well; it was noon.

A Samaritan woman came to draw water.
Jesus said to her, "Give me a drink."
(His disciples had gone to the town to buy food.)
– "How can you, a Jew, ask me –
    A Samaritan woman – for a drink?"
(Jews do not mingle with Samaritans.)
– "If you only were aware of God's gift **to you** –
    Who it was who asked you for a drink
    You would have asked him for something in return, and
    He would have giving you living water."
– "Sir, but you have no pail and the well is deep,
    How can you give me living water?
    Are you greater than our father, Jacob, who gave us this well,
    And drank from it himself, as did his sons and cattle?"
– "Everyone who drinks of this water will be thirsty again,
    But whoever drinks of the water I give will never thirst.
    Indeed, the water I give him will become in him
    A fountain of water welling up to life eternal."
– "Sir, give me this water so that I will not thirst again.
    And no longer need to come here to draw water."[2]

---

[1] This seems to be an attempt by an editor to remove the suggestion that Jesus
was competing with John.
[2] Is she stupidly missing the point or is she mocking Jesus?

– "Go, fetch your husband and return."
– "I have no husband."
– "You speak the truth when you say you have no husband;
   You have had five husbands in the past but the one
   You have now is not your husband; you tell the truth."
– "Sir, I see that you are a prophet,
   Our ancestors worshipped on this mountain but
   You say that Jerusalem is the place where one must worship."[1]
– "Believe me, woman, the time is coming when neither on
   This mountain nor in Jerusalem will you worship the Father.
   You do not know what you worship, but we do know,
   For it is from the Jews that deliverance will come.
   Yet the time is coming, indeed it has already come when
   True worshippers will worship the Father in the spiritual and
      earthly worlds[2];
   Such are the worshippers the Father seeks.
   God is spirit and his worshippers must worship him in the
      spiritual and earthly world.
– "I know the Messiah (called Christ) is coming;
   When that one comes, he will explain all."
– "I, who speak to you, am he."

At that moment, the disciples returned to him.
They were surprised to find him speaking to the woman,
But no one asked her, "What do you want?"
Nor him, "Why do you speak to her?"
The woman left behind her water jug and went into the town.
She told the townsfolk, "Come and see a man who told me
Everything I ever did. Is he not the Messiah?"
They left the town to go to him.

---

[1] The Samaritans had their shrine in Samaria.

[2] The Greek text has 'in spirit and truth'; but what does this mean? The modern translations do not help as most translate literally. J.B. Phillips (1958) translates 'in spirit and reality'; James Moffatt (rev. 1935): 'in Spirit and reality'. Both suggest that we are being told to worship God in the two worlds of heaven and earth, a view I share; hence the translation: 'in the spiritual and earthly worlds'.

Meanwhile, the disciples urged him: "Rabbi, eat something."
He said, "I have food to eat of which you have no inkling."
The disciples asked each other, "Has anyone brought him
    food?"
– "My food is to do the will of he who has sent me
    and to complete his work; and do not say,
'It is yet four months until the time of harvesting.'
Indeed, I tell you, Open your **spiritual** eyes and
Look at the fields **of human souls;** they are ripe for harvest;
The reaper is already drawing his wages and
Gathering the crop for life eternal,
So that the sower rejoices with the reaper.
The proverb 'one sows and another reaps' is true:
I sent you to reap a crop for which you did not work;
Others did the work[1] and you have benefited from their labour."

Now, many Samaritans from the town believed in him
Because of the evidence of the Samaritan woman:
"He told me all that I had ever done."
So, when the Samaritans approached him, they asked him
To remain with them, which he did for two days.
Through his teachings, many more became believers.
They said to the woman, "We no longer just believe
Because of what you told us. Now that we have heard him,
We know that this man is truly the Saviour of the World.[2]

Jesus performs a second miracle in Cana

After two days, he left for Galilee. Jesus had said,
"A prophet has no honour in his own country," yet when
He arrived in Galilee, he was warmly welcomed;
The Galileans knew what he did in Jerusalem during the
    festival,

[1] Is this a reference to John the Baptiser and the prophets who predicted the coming of the Messiah?

[2] They recognise St. Paul's view of Jesus as being far more than the Messiah of the Jews

For they too had gone there to celebrate the festival.
Once again he visited Cana in Galilee where he had changed
the water into wine;
A royal official was there whose son lay ill in Capernaum;
On hearing that Jesus had arrived in Galilee from Judea,
He came and begged him to come to heal his son
For he was about to die. So Jesus told him,
"Unless you witness signs and wonders, you will not believe."
– "Please Sir, come down before the child dies."[1]
– "Go, your son will live."
The man believed in what Jesus had said and left.
On the way home, his servants met him
And told him that his son was alive;
When he asked about the time of his recovery, they said,
"Yesterday at one in the afternoon, the fever abated."
The father calculated that that was the time
Jesus had said to him, "Your son will live."
So he and his entire household believed.
This was now the second sign that Jesus performed
After coming down from Judea into Galilee.

5 Jesus heals a cripple on the Sabbath
He speaks of his power to give eternal life

After this, Jesus went up to Jerusalem for a Jewish festival.
In Jerusalem by the Sheep Gate is a pool with five porticoes,
    known in Hebrew as Bethzatha.
In the porticoes lay many disabled people:
The blind, the lame and those with shrivelled limbs.
Among them was a man who had been afflicted for thirty-eight
    years.
When Jesus, knowing the length of his condition, asked him,
"Do you not wish to get well?"

---

[1] The official avoids engaging in a theological debate; he only asks for his son's life.

– "Sir, there is nobody to put me into the pool when the water
    stirs.[1]
  When I try to enter on my own,
  Someone pushes in before me."
– "Up, lift up your mat and walk!"
Instantly, he was made whole; he took his mat and walked.
That day, being the Sabbath, the Jews said to the healed man:
"It is the Sabbath; you are not permitted to carry the mat."
– "The man who healed me said to me, 'Take your mat and
    walk.'"
– "Who told you, 'Take your mat and walk'?"
The healed man did not know who it was as
Jesus had merged into the large crowd.

Later, Jesus met him at the Temple and said to him,
"Ah, you are totally well again; sin no more,
  Lest something worse happen to you."
So the man went and told the Jews that Jesus had healed him.[2]
The Jews hounded Jesus because he did this on the Sabbath.[3]
Jesus said, "My father works even now, as I work too."
Because of this they were even more intent on killing him –
Not only was he breaking the Sabbath, but by calling God
His father, he was making himself equal to God.
Jesus answered this: "In truth, I say to you,
The Son cannot act on his own, but only by what he sees
His father doing; whatever he does, the Son also does;
For the Father loves the Son and shows him all he does.

[1] A mineral pool which on occasion bubbled?
[2] As most of the inhabitants of Judea are Jews, it is obvious that the man went
to a certain group of Jews. The fact that St. John implicates all Jews in the
story indicates his antisemitic bias – the collectivisation of Jewish guilt. It is
important to be able to recognise the virtues of the gospel without ignoring his
great failings, for which, to its considerable credit, the Catholic Church, in its
apology to the Jewish community for its historical prejudice, has acknowledged.
[3] Is it possible that all the Jews would have persecuted Jesus for his miraculous
cures on the Sabbath or because he was claiming that God had granted him all
his power?

"He will reveal to you even greater works than these,
So that you may marvel; as the Father raises the dead and
Gives them life, even so does the Son give life to his chosen.
For the Father judges no one; he has handed over
The power of judgement to the Son, so that all men should
Honour the Son as they honour the Father.
He who does not honour the Son
Honours not the Father who sent him.
In truth, I tell you: He who hears me and believes in him
That sent me has life eternal and will not be judged.
He has already made the crossing from death into life.[1]
In truth I tell you, the time is coming, even now,
When the dead who hear the voice of the Son of God –
Those who hear will live.
As the Father has the life-giving power in himself,
So has he granted the life-giving power to the Son;
He has given him the authority to judge because
He is the Son of Man. Do not marvel at this:
That the time is coming when all who are in their graves will
Hear his voice and come out; those who have done good –
To the resurrection for life; those who have done evil –
To the resurrection for judgement.
By myself, I do nothing; as I hear, so do I judge.
My judgement is just, for my desire is not to please myself
But him who sent me.[2]

"If I give witness to prove myself, my testimony is invalid.
There is another person who is my witness whose testimony
I know is true; you have sent to John to act as my witness.
His testimony I know to be the truth.
I do not require human proof, but I tell you this so that

---

[1] The implication is that believers will not suffer death as St. Paul wrote in
1 Corinthians, 15:51

[2] It is unlikely that Jesus would have uttered these words, as he would have
been arrested for heresy. One needs to refer to *Luke* 22:66–71 to appreciate St.
John's articulation of Pauline Christianity.

You may be saved. That man was a bright burning lamp
And for a time you delighted in the joy of his light.
But, I have a greater witness than John:
The very work the Father has given me to finish –
The work that I am doing – gives witness to me that
The Father has sent me. The Father who has sent me has
Himself given testimony about me.[1]

"You have neither heard his voice or seen his form.
Neither does his word reside in you because you do not
Believe in the one whom he has sent.
You search through the Scriptures because you think that
Through them, you will achieve eternal life.
But, these Scriptures testify about me;
Yet you have no desire to come to me to have life.
I do not receive glorification from men, but I know you.
There is no love of God in you.
I come in the name of the Father, but you do not accept me.
But, if someone comes by his own authority, you accept him.
How can you believe if you glorify each other,
Yet do not seek glory that comes from the only God?
Think not that I will accuse you before the Father;
Moses, in whom you have hoped, accuses you.
If you believed Moses, you would believe me,
For it was about me that he wrote.[2]
But if you do not believe what he wrote,
How can you believe what I say?"

---

[1] The Father's testimony is the miraculous powers given to Jesus, similar to those granted to Moses.

[2] Moses never prophesied a Messiah, as he did not support a human monarchy, nor the coming of the Son of God who would bestow eternal life on those who believed in him. He did, however, prophesy the coming of a prophet, see p. 11 fn. 2.

6 The miracle of the loaves and fishes

After this, Jesus crossed to the farther shore of the
Sea of Galilee (Tiberius) where a large crowd followed him;
For they had seen the signs he had performed on the cripples.
Jesus went up the hillside where he sat with his disciples.
It was near Passover, the Jewish festival.
Jesus looked up and saw the large crowd approaching him.
He asked Philip: "Where are we to buy bread for these people
   to eat?"[1]
This was only to test him, for he knew what he would do.
Philip replied, "Two hundred denarii[2] would not buy enough to
   give each of them even a biteful."
One of his disciples, Andrew, Simon Peter's brother, said,
   "There is a boy here with five barley loaves and two fishes;
   But how will this help to feed so many of them?"
Jesus said, "Tell the people to sit down."
There was plenty of grass on which some five thousand men
   sat down.
Jesus took the loaves and, after giving thanks,
Gave as much as they wanted to the seated crowd.
He did the same with the fish.
Now, when they were full up, he told his disciples,
"Collect the left-over bits so that nothing is wasted."
They collected the leftovers and filled twelve baskets
With the remains of the five barley loaves they had eaten.
When the people saw this sign performed by Jesus, they said,
"Truly this is the Prophet who is to come into the world."[3]
Jesus, aware that they would soon come and take him
To make him king, withdrew on his own to the hills.

In the evening, his disciples went down to the sea

---

[1] Jesus had no responsibility to feed them, but it is an opportunity to prove himself, as did Moses on giving mannah to the Israelites.

[2] One dinarius was the daily wage for a manual labourer.

[3] In 1:21 John is asked whether he is the prophet. See p. 11 fn. 2. The prophet foretold by Moses and the Messiah-King foretold by Isaiah coalesces here.

And set off across the lake for Capernaum.
It was dark but Jesus had not yet joined them.
A strong wind blew, creating great waves;
Having rowed some twenty-five to thirty furlongs,
They saw Jesus walking on the sea, approaching the boat.
They were frightened, but he reassured them,
"It is I, do not be afraid."
They wanted to take him on to the boat,
But the boat had already landed at their destination.

Jesus is the source of eternal life
He is the mannah from heaven

The next day, the crowd standing on the opposite shore
Saw the one boat that had been there and knew that
Jesus had not embarked on it with his disciples,
But they had departed alone without him.
Some boats from Tiberius landed near the place where
They had eaten bread after the Lord had given thanks.
When the crowd realised that neither Jesus nor his disciples
Were there, they embarked into the boats and came to
Capernaum to search for Jesus. Finding Jesus across the lake,
They asked him, "Rabbi, when did you get here?"[1]
Jesus relied to them. "In truth I tell you, you look for me
Not because of the signs I performed, because having eaten the
    loaves, you were satisfied.
Do not struggle for food that perishes
But for the food that brings eternal life,
Which the Son of Man will give you.
On him, God the Father has imprinted his seal."
– "What is the work of God that we must do?"
– "The work that God requires is this:
    Believe in the one whom he has sent."
– "What sign will you perform that we may see

---

[1] Interestingly, they do not call him prophet or proclaim him king, as he feared.

And so believe you. What will you do?
Our forefathers ate manna in the wilderness as it says,
'He gave them bread out of heaven to eat.' "[1]
– "In truth I tell you,
It is not Moses who gave you bread from heaven,
But it is my father who gives you the true bread from
   heaven.
For the bread of God is he who comes down from heaven
And gives life to the world."
– "Sir, give us this bread forever."
– "I am the bread of life,"
He who comes to me will never again be hungry;
He who believes in me will never again be thirsty.
But I told you: you have seen me; yet, do not believe.
Whomever the Father has decided to give to me will come;[2]
And I will never drive out whomsoever comes to me.
For, I have not come down from heaven to do my will
But to obey the will of him who sent me.
And this is the will of him who sent me:
That I lose not any of those whom he granted to me
But shall raise them up at the end of days;
For it is my father's will that whosoever sees the Son
And believes in him shall have life eternal,
For I will raise him up at the end of days."

The Jews began to mutter[3] against him because he said,
"I am the bread that has come down from heaven."
For they said, "Is this man not Jesus the son of Joseph,

---

[1] This dialogue is full of irony. Having seen the miracle of the loaves and fishes, they declared him to be the prophet foretold by Moses. Now they want another miracle to make them believe. They cite bread from heaven given to their ancestors, but they know that neither manna nor the other miracles were sufficient to make the Israelites faithful.

[2] This suggests the Pauline concept of grace.

[3] The Jews are portrayed as following the example of the Israelites who were recorded as always 'murmuring' against Moses in spite of all the signs and wonders he performed for them.

Whose father and mother are known to us; how can he say,
'I have come down out of heaven?'"
Jesus said, "Stop muttering amongst yourselves.
No one comes to me unless the Father who sent me chooses him.
Him will I raise up at the end of days.
As it is written in the *Prophets*,[1]
"They shall all be taught by God."[2]
Everyone, who listens and learns from the Father, comes to me.
No one has seen the Father except the one coming from God;
Only he has seen the Father. In truth I tell you:
He who believes has life eternal.
I am the bread of life.
Your forefathers ate manna in the wilderness; yet died.
This is the bread coming down from heaven
Which a man may eat and not die.
I am the bread of life that came down from heaven.
If a man eats of this bread, he will live forever.
The bread is my flesh which I give for the life of the world."

He who eats the flesh of Jesus and drinks his blood becomes part of him as he is part of the Father

The Jews began to quarrel fiercely among themselves,
"How can this man give us his flesh to eat?"[3]
"In truth I tell you," said Jesus to them,
"Unless you eat the flesh of the Son of Man
And drink his blood, you have no life in yourselves,
But whoever eats my flesh and drinks my blood
Has life eternal; I will raise him up at the end of days.

[1] *Isaiah* 54:13.

[2] Through his prophets.

[3] If there was a fierce quarrel, it had to consist of one group who supported Jesus maintaining that he was speaking figuratively and the other: the mockers whose words are quoted. St. John is prepared to sacrifice literary integrity in order to achieve the wholesale condemnation of the Jews.

For my flesh is true food and my blood true drink.[1]
Whoever eats my flesh and drinks my blood
Becomes part of me and I of him.
Just as the Father sent me and I live through the Father,
Whoever eats me will live through me.
This is the bread that came down from heaven,
Not that which our forefathers ate and yet died –
Those who eat this bread will live forever."[2]
He said this while teaching in a synagogue in Capernaum.
On hearing this, many of his disciples said,
"This is a difficult teaching; who can accept it?"[3]
Jesus, aware that his disciples were muttering about this,
Said to them, "Does this offend you? What if you were to see
The Son of Man ascend to where he was before?
The Spirit gives life; the flesh gives nothing of any worth.
The words I have spoken are of the Spirit; they are life![4]
But there are some of you who do not believe."
Jesus had know from the beginning those who did not believe;
And the one who would betray him. So he said to them:
"That is why I told you that no one can come to me
Unless it was through the gift[5] of the Father."
At this, many of his disciples turned their backs on him

---

[1] Some translators understandably render 'real' rather than 'true'. I prefer the latter as it allows for more ambiguity, for how does one define 'real'? Socrates maintained that only ideas were real as they were the foundation stones of our comprehension of physical objects. It is likely that St. John had such a definition in mind when he put these words into the mouth of Jesus.

[2] Jesus is articulating the dogma of Pauline Christianity – as impressive as it is shocking: men and women become immortal by becoming part of God the Son and God the Father through eating the flesh of Jesus and drinking his blood.

[3] This is not surprising. In the perspective of life and thought in Judea, such a concept would have been so totally foreign as to be beyond belief.

[4] Is John here explaining that Jesus was speaking figuratively about eating his flesh? What Jesus is demanding is total identification with him through the faith that he, as the Son of Man, is also the Son of God who has come to save humanity from the corruption of earthly flesh.

[5] This is the gift of grace of which St. Paul writes. Even the capacity for faith is not within an individual's power. Even it is a gift from God. This too is a hard teaching.

And no longer followed him. Jesus asked the Twelve,
"Do you also want to go?" It was Simon Peter who answered,
"Lord, to whom else shall we go?
You have the teaching of life eternal;
We believe and know that you are God's Holy One."
Then Jesus said, "Have I not chosen you – the twelve of you?
But one of you is a devil." He was referring to Judas,
The son of Simon Iscariot, one of the Twelve,
Who would betray him.

7 Jesus at the Temple

Following this, Jesus kept himself to Galilee;
He did not want to go to Judea since
The Jews there were intent on killing him.
When the Jewish festival of Tabernacles drew near,
His brothers said, "You ought to leave here and go to Judea
So that your disciples may witness your powers,
For, if you wish to become famous, you cannot act secretly.
If you do such things, you must show yourself to the world."
For his brothers did not believe in him.[1] So Jesus retorted,
"My time has not yet come, for you any time is right.
The world has no reason to hate you, but it hates me
Because I declare that what it does is evil.
You go up to celebrate the festival. I will not go up
For the festival because my time has not yet come."

Having said this, he remained in Galilee.
But, after his brothers went up, he also went up,
Not to reveal himself but as a private individual.
During the festival, the Jews were looking for him, asking,
"Where is that man?" There was much muttering about him
Among the crowds; some were saying, "He is a good man."
Others said, "No, he misleads people."

---

[1] Had they believed in him, they would know that he did not need to publicise himself; they are being contemptuous of his claims.

No one[1], however, spoke honestly about him
Because of their fear of the Jews.[2]

It was not until the middle of the festival week that
Jesus went into the Temple to teach. The Jews were amazed:
"How did this unlettered man achieve such learning?"
– "My teaching is not my own,
  But of the one who sent me; if anyone wishes to do his will,
  He should know whether the teaching derives from God,
  Or whether I speak for myself.
  He who speaks on his own
  Seeks to gain honour for himself,
  But he who seeks honour for the one who sent him
  Is a man of truth – there is no deceit in him.
  Has not Moses given you the Law?
  Yet not one of you keeps the Law.[3]
  Why are you seeking to kill me?"
– "You are possessed by a demon. Who seeks to kill you?"
– "I performed one miracle;
  You were all amazed **but angry as it was on the Sabbath.**
  Yet, because Moses ordained circumcision – though in fact,
  It did not begin with Moses but with the patriarchs.
  If you circumcise a child on the Sabbath so as not
  To break the Law of Moses, why are you angry with me
  For healing an entire man[4] on the Sabbath?[5]
  Stop making petty judgements; judge properly."

[1] Those who fully believed in him.
[2] As they were all Jews, this is a gratuitous reference, which must have helped
to demonise the Jews among Christians.
[3] In what sense do they break the Law: by their intent to murder him?
[4] While circumcision is work, this commandment supersedes the law of not
working on the Sabbath. Jesus maintains, that if it is proper to heal one part of
the body on the Sabbath (though some would not view circumcision in that
light), it must be permitted to heal the entire body on the holy day.
[5] The narrative implies that the reason for wanting to kill him is his cure of the
cripple at Bethzatha on the Sabbath. The heresy of his claiming equality with God
was a far worse crime but, as he preached this in Capernaum in Galilee, news of it

Is Jesus the Prophet or the Messiah

Then some of the Jerusalemites asked,
"Is not this the man they are seeking to kill?
Yet he now speaks openly and no one objects;
Have our rulers decided that he indeed is the Messiah?
But we know where the man is from but the tradition is that,
When the Messiah comes, no one will know his origin"[1]
When Jesus, who was still teaching in the Temple, heard this,
He cried out, "You and I both know where I am from but,
I am not here by my own accord,
But the Faithful One has sent me.
You do not know him, but I know him
Because I come from him who sent me."
At this they wanted to seize him,
But no one laid a hand on him
Because his time had not yet come.
Many from the crowd believed in him because they asked,
"When the Messiah comes, will he do more signs than he has?"
The Pharisees heard the crowd muttering over these matters,
The chief priests and the Pharisees sent guards to arrest him.

Jesus, therefore, said, "I am with you for only a short time,
And then I go to him who has sent me. You will look for me,
But you will not find me; and where I go, you cannot come."
The Jews spoke among themselves,
"Where is this man going, so that we will not find him?
Is he going to the Diaspora to teach the Greeks?
What did he mean when he said,
'You will seek but not find me;
Where I go you cannot come?"[2]

---

would not have reached Jerusalem. Of course, it would have been incredible for
Jesus to have articulated this later interpretation of his mission to earth.

[1] The suggestion here is that the desire to kill him is not because he healed on
the Sabbath but because he was a false Messiah.

[2] Rightly, they could not comprehend the return of a Messiah to God. They
speculated on his going to direct his message to the Jews who lived in the Roman
Empire among the Hellenists, as his own countrymen were rejecting him.

On the last and most important day of the festival,
Jesus stood and cried out, saying,
"If anyone thirsts, let him come to me –
He who believes in me – let him drink!
'Streams of living waters will flow from him,'
Say the Scriptures."
This he said in regard to the Spirit,
Which would be received
By those who believed in him;
The Spirit had not yet been given,
As Jesus had not yet been glorified.[1]
On hearing his words, some said,
"Surely, he is the Prophet;"
Others said, "He is the Messiah."[2]
But others asked, "Can the Messiah be from Galilee?
Do not the Scriptures say that the Messiah comes from David,
From Bethlehem, the town where David lived?"[3]

The crowd were divided over Jesus.
Some were keen to arrest him, but no one laid hands on him.
When the guards returned to the chief priests and Pharisees,
And were asked by them, "Why did you not bring him in?"
– "Never has a man spoken as has this man,"
– "So, you have also been deceived," responded the Pharisees.
Do any of the rulers or Pharisees believe in him? No!

---

[1] The gift of eternal life could come only to those who believed in his resurrection. For St John, as for St. Paul, Jesus's messianic role as king of Israel is peripheral to his divine nature, which is granted to those who have faith in his divinity.

[2] They argue whether he is the Prophet or the Messiah, but not the Son of God who is destined for death and resurrection, which would have been beyond their comprehension, as it was beyond that of his disciples.

[3] This problem is addressed by the synoptic gospels, who have Jesus born in Bethlehem, though his parents live in Nazareth.

But the crowd who do not know the Law are cursed."
Nicodemus, who had gone to Jesus earlier,
But was one of them, asked,
"Does our Law judge a man without first hearing him and
Ascertaining what he has done?"
– "Are you too from Galilee? Consider and appreciate
   That a prophet never comes from Galilee."

8 The woman caught in adultery

[They all left, each to his own home.
But Jesus went to the Mount of Olives.
At dawn, he again went to the Temple.
All the people came to him;
They sat down and he taught them.
Now the Scribes and the Pharisees
Led in a woman caught in adultery.
They stood her up in front of them,
And said to Jesus, "Teacher, this woman has been caught
   in the act of committing adultery;
Now in our Law, Moses commanded that this woman be
   stoned.
Now, what do you say?" They said this to trap him,
To have another excuse to accuse him.
Jesus, stooping down, wrote on the ground with his finger.
But as they kept questioning him, he stood erect and said,
"He of you who is sinless – let him cast the first stone."
Again stooping down, he wrote on the ground.
Then, all those who heard him drifted away,
One by one, the older ones first; he was left on his own,
But the woman still stood there.
Standing up, Jesus said to her,
   "Woman, where are they?
   Has no one condemned you?"
– "No one, Sir."
– "Then,

35

I do not condemn you;
Go and sin no more."]¹

Jesus is the Light of the world; those who accept his teaching will not know death

Jesus spoke again to the Pharisees,
"I am the light of the world,
He who follows me will never walk in darkness,
But will have the light of life."
– "You give witness to yourself; such testimony is invalid."²
– "Though I am my own witness, my testimony is valid
   Because I know from where I came and where I go.
   But you do not know from where I came and where I go.
   You judge according to human moral standards;
   I do not judge anyone but, were I to pass judgement,
   My judgement would be true because I am not alone,
   But I am with the one who sent me. In your³ own Law
   It is written that the testimony of two witnesses is valid.
   I bear witness to myself, and the Father who sent me
   Bears witness to me."
– "Where is your father?"⁴
– "You neither know me nor my father
   For, if you knew me, you would also know my father."
He spoke these words in the Treasury,⁵
The place where he taught in the Temple.
No one seized him because his time had not yet come.⁶

---

¹ The authoritative manuscripts omit 7:53–8:11, which is the story of Jesus and the adulterous woman. Even though it is considered to be a later insertion, it is too wonderful to miss.
² They use Jesus's very words when he claims above that not he but John the Baptiser is his valid witness.
³ Jesus would not have distanced himself from the Torah by calling it 'your' Law.
⁴ They want to see him and hear his testimony.
⁵ The place where the people made their financial donations.
⁶ While St. John is perhaps the most anti-Jewish of the gospels, here and throughout the narrative he exonerates the Jews of responsibility for killing

He spoke again to them, "I go and you will seek me;
You will die in your sin. Where I go, you cannot come.
The Jews, therefore, wondered, "Is he to kill himself,
As he says, 'Where I go, you cannot come?'" But he said,
"You are from the world below, I am from the world above;
You are of this world; I am not of this world.
I told you that you would die in your sinfulness,
For if you do not believe in who I am,
You will die in your sinfulness."
– "Who are you, then?"
– "What point is there in my speaking to you?[1]
   I could say a lot about you and could judge you harshly.
   But I **will only say that** the one who sent me is true;
   I declare to the world only what I have heard from him."
They were not aware that he was speaking about the Father.
Jesus said, "When you lift up the Son of Man,[2]
Then you will know who I am, that of myself I do nothing.
I only speak that which the Father has taught me.
He who sent me is with me.
He never leaves me because I always do what pleases him."
As he spoke, many began to believe in him.
He said to the Jews who believed in him,
"If you accept my teaching, you are my true disciples;
You will know the truth and the truth will make you free."
– "We are the descendants of Abraham,
   And we have never been enslaved to anyone,[3]

---

him, as he had to die to fulfil the Christian mystery. The Jews were just God's tool for doing his will. One is reminded that God hardens Pharoah's heart in order to give himself the opportunity to display his power by performing more miracles. This is inherent in myths of redemption, both in that of a people, the Exodus, and an individual, the Son of God: miracles are required to inspire faith.

[1] He has told them enough times of his divine mission.

[2] When they put him on the cross and realise that he is the Son of God.

[3] This is a boastful statement from people who had been in servitude under the yoke of Egypt, Babylon, Persia, Hellas and Rome. They could have only meant in a spiritual sense.

How then can you say, 'You will be free?'"
– "In truth I tell you,
  Anyone who behaves sinfully is a slave to sin.
  Now, a slave does not stay in the house[1] forever,
  But the Son is there forever; so, if the Son sets you free,
  You will, indeed, be free. I know you are Abraham's seed,
  Yet, you seek to kill me[2] because there is no room in you for
    my teaching.
  I speak of what I have seen from the Father.
  Therefore, obey what you have heard from your father."
– "Abraham is our father,"
– "If you are Abraham's children, you would follow his
    example,
  But you are seeking to kill me, a man who has spoken
  The truth to you – that which I heard from God.
  Abraham did not do this. You are acting as your father."[3]
– "Our birth is not out of promiscuity,
  The only father we have is God."[4]
– "If God was your father, you would love me;
  I am and come from God;
  I have not come out of my own accord; he sent me.
  Why will you not understand what I say?
  It is because you cannot comprehend my teaching.

[1] This must mean the house of eternal life, for a slave has as much permanence
in a household as members of the family, though Hebrew slaves were released
on Sabbatical years.

[2] This is strange because he is speaking to the Jews who believe in him.
Equally, there is no evidence that they do want to kill him, except rumour.
Previously, when Jesus makes this accusation, he himself is accused of being
obsessed: "Who wants to kill you?" 7:20

[3] Is Jesus referring to Abraham's hospitality of the three men sent by God to tell
him of the birth of Isaac? He is saying that, rather than acting like the
Patriarch, they are behaving as badly as their father, who is later identified as
the devil.

[4] This is very confusing; these words would more appropriately have come
out of the mouth of Jesus himself. It has been suggested that this is a
personal attack on Jesus's mother who was pregnant before her marriage to
Joseph.

– "Your father is the devil and you wish to meet his desires.[1]
  He was a murderer from the beginning;
  He does not accept the truth for truth is not in him.
  When he lies, he speaks out of his own nature
  Because he is a liar and the father of lies.
  But, because I speak the truth, you do not believe.
  Who of you can reprove me for any sin?[2]
  If I speak the truth, why do you not believe me?
  He who is of God understands the words of God.
  Since you do not understand, you are not of God."

The Jews retaliated, "Are we not right to say that
You are a Samaritan and possessed by a demon?"
– "I am not a demon;
  I honour my father and you dishonour me.
  I do not seek glory for myself;
  There is one who seeks it, who passes judgement.
  In truth, I tell you: if a man holds onto my teaching,
  He will never see death."
– "Now we know that
  You are possessed by a demon.
  Abraham died as did the prophets and you say,
  'If a man holds on to your teaching,
  He will never taste death.'
  Are you greater than our father, Abraham?
  He died, as did the prophets.
  Who do you claim to be?"
– "If I make claims of glory for myself, my glory is nothing.
  My father, who you say is our God, is he who glorifies me.
  You have not known him, but I know him.
  If I said that I do not **in order to please you,**

---

[1] The debate turns into a demeaning slanging match. St. John loses his
credibility here. In the demonisation of the Jews, he also denigrates the stature
of Jesus who appears to relish the confrontation, even with those who began
by being sympathetic to his charisma.
[2] i.e., not telling the truth.

I would be a liar like you,[1] but I do know him
And obey his teaching.
Abraham, your father, was glad to think of my day –
The day of my coming. He saw it and rejoiced."
– "You are not fifty years old,
   And you have seen Abraham?"[2]
– "In truth I tell you, before Abraham was born I existed."[3]
They, therefore, collected stones to throw at him,[4]
But Jesus hid and escaped from the Temple.

9 The man born blind was to reveal God's glory through Jesus

Once, he saw a man who had been blind since birth.
"Rabbi, who sinned", asked his disciples,
"The man or his parents as he was born blind?"
– "Neither this man nor his parents sinned,
   But that the works of God might be revealed through him.
   While it is yet day, we must do the work of him who sent
      me.
   When night comes, no one is able to work.
   When I am in the world, I am the light of the world."
Saying this, he spat on the ground, made clay with the
   saliva
And put the clay on the man's eyes. "Go", he told him,
"Wash in the pool of Siloam (meaning 'having been sent')."
He went and washed and returned with full sight.

---

[1] St. John portrays Jesus as being highly provocative, particularly in the light of a radically new teaching which would have been very foreign to traditional thought.

[2] He never said that he saw Abraham.

[3] This would have been equating himself with God – a highly inflammatory statement.

[4] As they felt that Jesus was possessed by a demon, it is unlikely that they would have decided to stone a madman, especially without the sanction of the authorities.

His neighbours who formerly knew him as a beggar said,
"Is this not the one who used to sit and beg?" Some said,
"It is he." Others: "No, but he looks like him."
He said, "I am the very same man." They asked him,
"How did you recover from your blindness?"
– "A man called Jesus made clay and put it over my eyes;
   He told me to go to the Siloam and wash; I went there
   And washed my eyes and then I could see."
– "Where is this man?"
– "I do not know."

They took the man who had been blind to the Pharisees.
It was a Sabbath when Jesus made the clay and restored his
   sight.
The Pharisees asked him again how he gained his sight.
He answered, "He put clay on my eyes, I washed and I saw."
Some of the Pharisees said, "This man cannot be from God
Because he breaks the Sabbath." But others asked,
"How can a sinner work such signs?" So they were divided.
They turned again to the blind man,
"What do you say about him, for it was your eyes he opened?"
He said: "He is a prophet."[1]

The Jews would not believe that he was blind and now saw;
They summoned his parents. "Is this your son," they asked,
"Is this the one you say was born blind; how can he now
   see?"
– "We know him to be our son who was born blind; but
   how he now sees and who opened his eyes we do not
   know;
Ask him for he is old enough to speak for himself."
This his parents said because they were afraid of the Jews
For the Jews had already agreed to excommunicate

---

[1] An astute observation, for it was only the legendary prophets, whose oracles are reported, notably Elijah and Elisha, who performed such miracles. There was no tradition of the Messiah being recognised by his performance of wonders.

Anyone who recognised Jesus as the Messiah.[1]

[2]They summoned the man who was blind a second time,
"Give glory to God, we know that this man is a sinner."[3]

– "I do not know whether Jesus is a sinner,
   One thing I do know is that I was blind and now I can see."

– "What did he do to you; how did he open your eyes?"

– "I have already told you but you would not listen.
   Why do you wish to hear it again – to become his disciples?"

– "You may be a disciple of that man,
   But we are disciples of Moses;[4]
   We know that through Moses, God spoke,
   But we do not know from where this man comes."

– "Now, that is remarkable: you do not know his origins,
   Yet he opened my eyes. We know that God does not hear
       sinners;
   He answers the god-fearing who obey his will.
   Never has it been heard that sight was given to one born
       blind.
   If this man was not from God, he could do nothing like
       this."

– "You who having been born wholly in sin, dare to teach
   us!"

They then cast him out.

Jesus heard that he had been cast out;
Finding him, he asked, "Do you believe in the Son of Man?"

– "Who is he Sir, that I may believe in him?"

– "You have seen him; he is speaking to you now."

---

[1] Historically, this was very unlikely, as the Jews were waiting for a Messiah to
break their Roman yoke of oppression. There were a number of false Messiahs,
but usually fighters.

[2] Now begins a brilliant debate full of humour between the Pharisees and the
cured blind person.

[3] 'Give glory to God' because it was he and not Jesus who cured him.

[4] There is no conflict between being a disciple of both. It was Paul, in his
letters, who feels compelled to show the superiority of Jesus to Moses; the latter
is mortal, the former eternal.

– "I believe, Sir." And he worshipped him.
And Jesus said,
"For judgement I came into this world;
That those who could not see will see
And that those who see will turn out to have been blind."
Some of the Pharisees who were with him heard this,
"Are we then also blind?"
– "If you were blind[1], you would not be guilty of sin.
  But, if you say, 'We see', then you remain in sin."

10 Jesus is the good shepherd[2]

"In truth I tell you, he who enters the sheep folds not
By the gate but by another way is a thief and a robber.
He who enters through the gate is the shepherd.
The gatekeeper opens the gate and the sheep obey him.
He calls his sheep by name as he leads them out.
When he leads them out, his sheep follow him because
They recognise his voice; they will never follow a stranger,
But run away from him because they do not know his voice."
Jesus told them this allegory, but they did not understand
The meaning of what he was saying to him.

Therefore, Jesus said again, "In truth I tell you:
I am the gate for the sheep; all who came before me were
Thieves and robbers[3] to whom the sheep would not listen.
I am the gate: whoever enters through me will be saved.
He will come in and go out and find pasture.
The thief comes only to steal, kill and destroy.
I came so that they may have life more abundant.
I am the good shepherd – the good shepherd

---

[1] I.e., ignorant of the truth of Jesus.
[2] The basis of this chapter could be *Ezekiel* 34 in which God describes himself as the shepherd of Israel who will appoint a Messiah from the House of David to rule his flock.
[3] Deceivers

Who lays down his life for the sheep.
The hired hand, not being the shepherd who owns the sheep,
When he sees a wolf coming leaves the sheep and runs away;
The wolf attacks them and they scatter.
Since he is but a hired hand, the sheep do not matter to him.

Jesus lays down his own life for his sheep
No one takes it away from him

"I am the good shepherd;
I know mine and they know me,
As the Father knows me and I know the Father.
I lay down my life for the sheep.
I have other sheep, which are not of this flock;[1]
I must bring them also to hear my voice
So there will be one flock and one shepherd.
The Father loves me because
I lay down my life in order to take it up again.
No one takes it from me,
But I myself lay it down.[2]
I have the authority to lay it down
And the authority to take it up again.
This mandate I received from my father."

A quarrel broke out among the Jews because of this teaching.
Many of them exclaimed, "He is possessed by a demon
And is raving; why do you listen to him? But others said,
"How can this be the teaching of a man possessed by a demon;
Can a demon open the eyes of the blind?"

---

[1] These can only be the Gentiles who are brought into the flock of Israel.
[2] This is surely proof that neither the Jews nor, for that matter, the Romans are responsible for Jesus's death, but he alone.

Jesus and the Father are one

It was the time of the Festival of Dedication[1] in Jerusalem.
It was winter; Jesus was walking in the Temple
  in Solomon's Colonnade.
The Jews surrounded him and asked:
"Until when will you keep us in suspense;
If you are the Messiah,[2] tell us plainly!"[3]
"I told you," answered Jesus, "but you do not believe:
The works I perform, I do in the name of my father,
And they bear witness to who I am, but you will not believe
Because you are not my sheep; my sheep hear my voice;
I know who they are and they follow me.
I give them life eternal and they shall never perish.
No one will snatch them from my hand.
My father, who has given them to me, is greater than all;
No one can snatch them out of the hand of the Father.
I and the Father are one."

Again, the Jews picked up stones to stone him. Jesus asked,
"I have shown you many good works which are from the
  Father;
For which of these good works will you stone me?"[4]
– "Not for a good work do we stone you, but for blasphemy –
  That you, a man, make yourself into God!"[5]

[1] The Jewish festival of Hanukkah, the celebration ascribed to the cleansing of the Temple after the successful revolution of the Hasmoneans against Antiochus 1V in 165 BCE.

[2] In this context: "Are you the one who has been anointed as king from the Davidic line to restore the sovereignty of Israel from under the Roman yoke?" In *Acts* 1, after Jesus's resurrection, his disciples ask him whether he has now returned "to restore the sovereignty of Israel". This was the Jewish expectation of the Messiah: to fulfil this expectation.

[3] He does answer plainly that he is the Messiah, but reverts to his miraculous signs and to the analogy with the shepherd mustering his flocks.

[4] Is Jesus inferring that they are stoning him for healing on the Sabbath?

[5] This is a proper insight: if the Jews under Roman rulers had the power to execute blasphemers, Jesus could have suffered such a fate, but in fact, Jesus was crucified not for this but for the civil crime of rebellion against Rome: his claim or that of his disciples that he was the anointed king of the Jews. This is

– "Is it not written in your Law:
  'I said, you are gods'?[1]
  If he called gods those who had God's word –
  And the truth of scripture cannot be denied –
  What of he whom God sanctified and sent into the world?
  Why do you say that I blaspheme because I said:
  I am the Son of God?[2]
  If I do not perform my father's works,
  Do not believe me.
  But if I perform these works,
  Even if you do not believe in me,
  Believe in the evidence of the works,
  So that you may continually know
  That the Father is in me and I am in him."[3]
Again they tried to arrest him,
But he escaped from their hands.[4]

He went away and again crossed the Jordan –
To the place where John first began to baptise.
He stayed there; many came to him.
They said, "John performed no signs,
But all that John said about this man is true."
In that place, many believed in him.

---

born out by the fact that, in the description of the Passion of Christ, the Jews and Jesus are portrayed as debating whether Jesus is the Son of God, but Pilate is only questioning him about his claim to being the Messiah – the king of Israel.

[1] The quote is not from the Law (the Torah) but from *Psalms 82:6*. The person speaking is God. Jesus would have made the distinction; why also does Jesus refer to it as 'your' rather than 'our' Law? In distancing Jesus from the Jews, St. John reveals an unhistorical Jesus, for was it not Jesus, according to St. Matthew, who attacks the Pharisees for crossing the seas to proselytise Gentiles instead of caring for the lost flock of Israel?

[2] But Jesus went further: he claimed that he and the Father were one.

[3] This is Pauline Christianity. Through faith in Christ, a believer through him becomes part of God which is the mystery of the Eucharist.

[4] This contradicts the report we just had that they were about to stone him without any authority.

11 Jesus raises Lazarus from the dead
Jesus is the resurrection and the source of life

Now there was a man called Lazarus who was ill.
Lazarus was from Bethany, the village where Mary and her
   sister Martha lived.
It was this Mary, whose brother Lazarus was ill, who
Anointed the Lord with oil and wiped his feet with her hair.[1]
The sisters sent for him, "Lord, he whom you love is ill."
When he heard this, he said,
"This illness will not bring death but the glory of God,
For through it the Son of God will be glorified."
Jesus loved Martha and her sister and Lazarus.
Though he heard that Lazarus was ill,
He stayed where he was for two more days.[2]
Then he said to his disciples, "Let us return to Judea."
– "But Rabbi, they were just now wanting to stone you
   And you are ready to return?"
– "Are there not twelve hours of daylight?
   A man who walks during the day does not stumble
   For he sees by this world's light.
   But if he walks at night,
   He stumbles because the light is not in him."[3]

But after this, he said, "Our friend Lazarus sleeps,
But I will go there to awaken him."
– "Lord, if he has fallen asleep, he will recover."
Jesus was referring to his death but they thought
He spoke of the sleep of slumber; so Jesus told them plainly,
"Lazarus is dead; but I rejoice for your sake that
I was not there so that you may now believe –

---

[1] This account is told in the next chapter.

[2] Without going to him.

[3] Jesus may be suggesting, that on this visit to Jerusalem, they will see the light
and not wish to stone him. In any event, Jesus has been sent to lay down his
life: the only question is the timing.

So let us go to him."[1] Then Thomas, called Didymus, said,
"Let us also go that we may die with him."[2]

On arrival, Jesus found that he had been buried for four days.
Bethany was about two miles from Jerusalem;
Many Jews had come to Martha and Mary to console them
   over their brother.
When Martha heard that Jesus had come she went to meet him;
Mary, however, stayed at home. Martha said to Jesus,
"Lord, if you had been here, my brother would not have died,
For I know that whatever you ask of God, he grants you."
– "Your brother will rise again."
– "I know he will rise again –
   In the resurrection at the end of days."
– "I am the resurrection and the source of life;
   He who believes in me, though he dies, will live;
   All who are alive and believe in me will never die.
   Do you believe this?"
– "Yes, Lord, I believe that you are the Messiah,
   The Son of God – he who was to come into the world."

Saying this, she went to speak privately to her sister Mary;
"The Teacher who is here summons you."
Hearing this, she immediately left to go to him.
Jesus had not yet entered the village,
But was at the place where Martha had met him.
The Jews who were consoling her in the house,
Seeing her departing so swiftly followed her;
They thought, "She is going to the tomb to weep there."
On reaching and seeing Jesus, Mary fell at his feet,
"Lord, if you had been here, my brother would not have died."
When Jesus saw her and the Jews with her weeping,

---

[1] The miracle of raising Lazarus from the dead would be more inspiring than raising him from the sick bed, especially if he had been buried for four days.
[2] Didymus means 'twin' in Greek, as the origin of the Hebrew name Thomas is Te'om which means twin. Thomas feels that Jesus is close to being executed and is prepared to die with him.

He was distressed and agitated, "Where have you put him?"
They appealed to him, "Come and see." Jesus wept.
The Jews said, "See how much he loved him!" But some said,
"Could not he who opened the eyes of the blind man
Have prevented this man from dying?"

Jesus, still deeply agitated, arrived at the tomb.
It was a cave with a stone covering it. Jesus said,
"Lift the stone." Martha, the sister of the dead man, said,
"Lord, by now he will smell for it is four days."
– "Did I not tell you that, if you believed in me,
    You would see the glory of God!"
They lifted the stone. Jesus looked up and said,
"Father I thank you that you have heard me;
I know that you always hear me,
But because of the crowd milling about me,
I said this so that they will believe that you sent me."
After saying this, with a loud voice, he cried out,
"Lazarus, come out." The dead man came out;
His hands and feet were swathed with bandages and his face
    bound by a napkin.
Jesus said to them, "Loosen him and let him go."

Caiaphas decides to sacrifice Jesus to save the Jews from the Romans

Many of the Jews who accompanied Mary,
Seeing this, believed in him; but some of them went to the
Pharisees to tell them what Jesus had done.
The chief priests and Pharisees assembled in council.
"What are we to do? This man is performing many signs.
If we ignore him, everyone will believe him.
The Romans will invade and destroy our Temple and nation."[1]

---

[1] This is a surprising insight: the recognition that the Jewish acceptance of
Jesus as the Messiah would be considered a rebellious act leading to the
destruction of the Jewish nation.

Caiaphas, who was the High Priest that year said to them,
"You understand nothing, nor realise that it is better for us
That one man should die for all the people,
Than that the whole nation perishes."
This view did not originate in himself[1] but, as High Priest,
He prophesied that Jesus was to die for the whole nation,
And not for the nation alone but for the children of God –
So that having been scattered he might gather them into one.[2]
From that day on they conspired to take his life.

Therefore, Jesus never walked freely among the Jews
But withdrew into the countryside near the desert to a village
    called Ephraim.
There he stayed with his disciples; when Passover drew near,
Many went up from the countryside to Jerusalem to purify
    themselves before Passover;
They looked for Jesus and spoke to each other in the Temple,
"What do you think? Will he not come to the festival at all?"
The chief priests and Pharisees gave orders that, if anyone
    knew where he was,
He should inform them, so that they could arrest him.

12 'The poor will always be with you But you will not always have me'

Six days before Passover, Jesus came to Bethany –
The home of Lazarus, whom Jesus raised from the dead.[3]

---

[1] A divine inspiration.

[2] This is the Pauline view of all humanity becoming one with God through the body of Christ, which is the Church – the holy community. The irony is that Jesus must be killed so that the Romans have no excuse to destroy the Jewish nation, but also to fulfil his mission of dying to redeem not only his fellow Jews but the entire world through his self-sacrifice. This means that, in plotting Jesus's death, the Jews are acting as God's agent in the unfolding of the divine mystery.

[3] In the gospels of *St. Matthew 26:6* and *St. Mark14:3* Jesus visits the home of Simon the leper and an anonymous woman pours precious oil on his head. As this story occurs in the three gospels before the Passover, it must derive from

They made supper for him, which Martha served,[1]
But Lazarus was eating with him;
Mary fetched a litre of pure and costly oil – spikenard;
She covered his feet with it and wiped them with her hair.
The house was filled with the fragrance of the perfumed oil.
Judas Iscariot, a disciple who was about to betray him said,
"Why was this oil not sold for three hundred denarii[2]
And given to the poor?"
He said this not because he cared for the poor,
But because he was a thief; he was in charge of the kitty
And would rifle the funds put into it.
Jesus said, "Leave her be, should she have waited to use it at
    my burial?
The poor will always be with you,
But you will not always have me."[3]

There was a large crowd of Jews who came not only because of Jesus,
But to see Lazarus whom he had raised from the dead.
The chief priests conspired also to kill Lazarus since
Many Jews had come to believe in Jesus because of him.
The next day, the large crowd, arriving for the festival,
Hearing that Jesus was coming to Jerusalem,
Gathered palm branches and went to meet him, crying out,
"Blessed be he who comes
In the name of the Lord –

---

an older source. In *St. Luke* 7:38, it is a prostitute who anoints his feet with
her tears and then oil before wiping them with her hair.

[1] In *St. Luke* 11:38,39 Jesus visits the home of Martha and Mary (there is no
mention of Simon the leper or Lazarus): there too, Martha serves and
complains that Mary does nothing but listen to the teachings of Jesus.

[2] As one denarius was the daily wage of a labourer, this was almost a year's
earnings for the poor. In the previously cited gospels, fn above, the other guests
or disciples are the moaners. Here, Judas is the sole kill-joy, an indication of his
own jealousy/frustration with Jesus as well as the attempt to demonise him for
his betrayal.

[3] *Deuteronomy* 15:11: "For the poor shall never cease to be in the land." This
observation is followed by the admonition to support them. Jesus is saying:
there is ample opportunity to win brownie points for giving charity but not
much time for showering love on him.

The very king of Israel."[1]
Seeing a young donkey, Jesus sat on it, as the Scriptures say,
"Fear not, O daughter of Zion;
See your king is coming,
Seated on the foal of a donkey."[2]
At first, the disciples did not understand its significance;
But, when Jesus was glorified, they realized that
This had been written about him – the very things
That had happened to him.
The crowd with him testified that he had summoned
Lazarus out of the tomb and raised him from the dead.
Many people, because they heard that he performed this sign,
Went to meet him. Then the Pharisees said to each other,
"See, it is too late to do anything; the world follows him."

The hour has come for the glorification of Jesus

There were Hellenists[3] among those who went up to worship
At the festival; they went to Philip of Bethsaida of Galilee,
And asked of him, "Sir, we wish to see Jesus."
Philip consulted Andrew[4]; both told Jesus. He said,
"The hour has come for the Son of Man to be glorified.[5]
In truth I tell you, unless a kernel of wheat
Falls to the ground and dies, it remains a seed alone.
But, if it dies, it bears much fruit.[6]
Thus, the man who loves his life, loses it and

---

[1] *Psalm* 118:25,26

[2] *Zechariah* 9:9, where the wording is different from the received text: "Rejoice fully, O daughter of Zion; shout, O daughter of Jerusalem. See your king comes to you; he is proven true and victorious. Humble – riding upon a donkey, even on a colt, the foal of a donkey." (my translation)

[3] If this approach was made in the Temple they could only have been Jews, whether born so or converted, living in the Diaspora because only Jews could enter the Temple. See *Acts 21:28*: Paul is falsely accused of bringing Hellenists into the Temple courts.

[4] Their concern is that they might betray Jesus.

[5] The time of his death and resurrection; therefore, they need not fear for his betrayal.

[6] By his death, Jesus will be accompanied into eternal life by all who believed in him.

The man who despises his life in this world
Will keep it for time eternal.
Let anyone who serves me follow me;
Where I am, there will my servant also be;
The Father will show him honour.

"My mind is agitated, for what can I say:
'Father, save me from this hour?'
But it was for this reason that my hour has come:
Father, glorify your name **through me.**"
A voice came out of heaven,
"I have glorified and I will glorify my name again."
The crowd who heard it said it was thunder;
Others said, "An angel spoke to him."
Jesus said, "This voice was not for me but for you,
Now is the hour of judgement for this world,
Satan, the ruler of this world is to be driven out.
And I, when I am lifted out of this world,
Will draw all men to myself."
He declared this to indicate the nature of the death he was
    going to die.

The people answered him,
"We know from the Law that the Messiah will remain forever,
So why do you say that the Son of Man must be lifted up.
Who is this Son of Man?"
Jesus told them, "The light is still among you for a while,
Walk while you have the light before darkness overtakes you;
The man who walks in darkness knows not where he goes.
While you have the light, believe in the light,
So that you may become sons of light."[1]
When he had finished speaking, he departed and hid himself.

Although he had performed so many signs before them,
They still did not believe in him, to fulfil Isaiah's word,

---

[1] Notice that he did not answer their question.

"Who would have believed our report?
And to whom has the strength[1]of the LORD been revealed?"
For this reason, they could not believe as Isaiah also says,[2]
"He has blinded their eyes and hardened their hearts,
That they might not see with their eyes
Nor understand with their hearts –
Lest they return that I might heal them."
Isaiah said this because he saw his glorification
And so was prophesying about him.

Yet, even so, many of the rulers believed in him,
But because of the Pharisees, did not confess to it,
In fear of being expelled from the community;[3]
They valued the praise of men more than the praise of God.

Then Jesus cried out, "He who believes in me not only
Believes in me but in the one who has sent me.
He who sees me also sees the one who has sent me.
I come into the world like a light so that everyone
Who believes in me does not remain in darkness.
He who hears my teaching without obeying it –
I do not judge him for I did not come to judge the world,
But that I might save the world.
For he who rejects me and does not accept my teaching,
There is one who judges him.
The word I spoke **which he rejected** will condemn him in
     judgement at the end of days.

[1] 53:1; here the Hebrew word implying strength is 'the arm'.
[2] This is a passage similar to but not identical to the traditional *Isaiah* 6:10.
What is significant here is the questionable behaviour of God or his Son in
compounding the sinfulness of the Jews by hardening their hearts to delay or
prevent their salvation until they have revealed their power through the
glorification of Jesus. But, it does have the effect of exonerating the Jews from
responsibility for his death.
[3] Literally: 'put out of the synagogue'; synagogue is a Greek word meaning
'place of assembly'. In this instance, it could not have been a matter of
expelling someone from synagogue membership, especially as the Temple was
the central place of worship.

I did not speak for myself; the Father who sent me gave me
  instructions on what I should say and how I should speak.
I know that in his commandment is life eternal.
Therefore, I say what the Father has told me to say."

13 Jesus washes the feet of his disciples

Before the festival of Passover, Jesus knew the hour
When he should leave this world to go to the Father.
He had loved his own in this world but now
He would reveal the full extent of his love.
Supper being served, and the devil having already
Seduced Judas Iscariot the son of Simon into betraying him.
Jesus knew that the Father had put him in full control,
That he had come from God and was returning to God –
He rose from the meal, stripped himself of his clothes
And wrapped a towel around his waist.
He put water into the basin and began to wash
The feet of his disciples and to dry them with the towel he had
  wrapped around himself.
When he came to Simon Peter, he protested:
"Lord, are you to wash my feet?"
– "You do not yet understand the meaning of what I now do,
  But you will comprehend in due course."
– "No, you shall never wash my feet."
– "Unless I wash you, you have no part in me."
– "Then Lord, not only my feet but also my head and hands."[1]
– "He who bathes is clean, only his feet need washing,
  You too are clean but not everyone of you."
For he knew the one who was to betray him;
Therefore he said, "Not everyone of you is clean."

---

[1] Peter wants to become an even greater part of him. Jesus responds by first
referring to physical cleanliness: (only feet require regular washing because of
the dust and perspiration from walking), but then to the spiritual: Judas is
unclean as he will betray him.

When he had finished washing their feet, he dressed himself
And, sitting down again, said to them,
"Do you understand why I have done this for you?
You call me Teacher[1] and Lord,
And rightly so, for that is what I am; now, therefore,
If I, your Lord and Teacher, wash your feet,
Should you not wash each other's feet?
I did this as an example, that you should do as I do.
In truth, I tell you, no servant is greater than his master,
Nor is a messenger greater than he who sent him.[2]
Once, you understand this, you will be blessed.

Satan enters Judas Iscariot

"In saying this I am not referring to all of you;
I know those whom I have chosen **and who are loyal.**
But **there is one here** to fulfil what is in the Scriptures:
'He who eats my bread has lifted up his heel against me.'[3]
I tell you this before it happens so that when it does.
You will believe who I am.[4] In truth, I tell you:
Whoever receives whom I send receives me and
He who receives me receives the one who sent me."
Then, Jesus was deeply agitated,
"In truth, I tell you: one of you is going to betray me."
The disciples looked at each other wondering about whom he
    spoke.

---

[1] Teacher and Rabbi are synonymous, for rabbi means 'master' which would have been the appellative of a teacher.

[2] Unless we understand this in the context that Jesus is both the master and the one who sends, and the disciples are the servants and the messengers, it makes no sense. If Jesus can wash their feet, they must make no distinction between themselves and others, but serve them as he, Jesus, had served them. The high-handed manner of Peter revealed in *Acts* would indicate that he did not take this advice

[3] *Psalms* 41:9; a descriptive introductory line in the verse is omitted: 'My own intimate friend whom I trusted . . .'

[4] His foreknowledge of the betrayer is one more indicator that he is the true Saviour.

One of them, who was dearest to Jesus, was sitting near him;
Simon Peter said to him, "Ask him of whom he is speaking."
Nestling close to Jesus, he asked him,
"Lord, who is it?"
– "It is the one to whom I give this piece of bread
    Once I have dipped it into the sauce."
He dipped the piece of bread and gave it to Judas Iscariot.
When he took the bread, Satan entered him. Jesus said to him,
"What you are about to do, do quickly."
No one sitting there understood to what Jesus was referring;
Since Judas was in charge of the kitty, Jesus was telling him
To buy things for the festival or to give to the poor.
Immediately after eating the bread, he left; it was night.

When he left, Jesus said,
"Now is the Son of Man to be glorified
And God is to be glorified through him,
For God will glorify the Son through himself;
He is to glorify him now.
Children, I am only with you for a little while;
You will look for me but, just as I told the Jews,[1]
So, I tell you, you cannot come to where I go.
I give you a new commandment: love one another!
As I have loved you, so must you love one another.
By loving one another all men will know that you are my disciples."

Simon Peter asked him, "Where are you going?"
– "Where I go, you cannot follow me now,
    But you will follow me later.",
– "Why cannot I follow you now?
    I will lay down my life for you."
– "Would you lay down your life for me?
    In truth I tell you, before the rooster crows,
    You will disown me three times."

---

[1] Were his disciples not Jews?

14 Jesus comforts his disciples

"Do not let your hearts be troubled.
Believe in God and believe in me.
In my father's house there are many rooms.
If not, I would have told you because
I am going to prepare a place for you;
After I go to prepare a place for you,
I will return and take you to myself;
That where I am, you will be and that
You know the way to where I go."

Thomas said to him,
    "Lord, we do not know where you go,
    So how can we know the way?"
– "I am the way and the truth and the life.
    No one comes to the Father except through me.
    If you had known me, you would have also known my
        Father.
    From now you will have known him and have seen him."
Philip said. – "Lord, show us the Father and that will be
    enough for us,"
– "Do you not understand me and
    I have been with you for such a long time?
    He who has seen me has seen the Father.
    How can you say, 'Show us the Father'?
    Do you not believe that I am in the Father and the Father is
        in me?
    The words I speak do not come from me;
    But from the Father in me who is fulfilling his work.
    Believe me: I am in the Father and the Father is in me.

Faith through the miracles
God will send a Comforter

"If you cannot believe because of what I tell you,
At least believe because of the miracles **I have performed.**

In truth I tell you, he who believes in me will be able to do
    what I have been doing;
He will do even greater things because I am returning to the
    Father;
Whatever you ask in My name, I will do,
So that the Father may be glorified in the Son.[1]
Anything you ask in my name,[2] I will do.

"If you love me, you will obey my commandments;
And I will ask the Father to give you another Comforter[3]
To always be with you – the Divine Spirit,[4]
Which the world cannot accept because
It neither sees it nor comprehends it;
But you know him[5]because he is in you and will be in you.
I will not leave you orphans; I will come to you.
In a little while the world will no longer see me,
But you will see me because as I live you will live.[6]
On that day, you will comprehend that I am in my Father
And you are in me and I am in you.
He who has my commandments and obeys them,

---

[1] This is extremely significant but conveniently forgotten by Christian believers
today. Jesus is promising that faith in him will give them the divine powers
that he possesses. Jesus is here giving authority to St. Paul's message that the
baptism in Christ instilled in his believers the divine spirit, which gave them
these powers: see *Acts*: 19:1–7. In *St. Luke*, a gospel influenced by St. Paul's
theology, Jesus gives The Twelve 'authority over demons and the power to heal
diseases' (9:1) Jesus appoints a further seventy-two and says to them, 'Heal
their sick and tell them: 'The Kingdom of God is coming closer to you.'(10:9)
[2] This is fulfilled according to *St Luke* 10:17: The seventy-two returned in a
state of euphoria. They told him (Jesus), "Even the demons surrender to us in
your name."
[3] Other translations are "counsellor, advocate, paraclete, protector".
[4] The literal translation is 'spirit of truth'. This is the translation used in most
bibles, but surely, based on what Jesus continues to say, it must be referring to
the divine spirit, which is what Jesus calls it later (14:25). This is in *him*
because he is the Son of God and in *them* through their identification with him.
This is the theological foundation of the Trinity. What unites the Father with
the Son and the Son with the faithful is the Holy Ghost (holy or divine spirit).
[5] 'It', the Divine Spirit, becomes "him", Jesus.
[6] i.e. after his crucifixion – through his resurrection and eternal life.

He is the one who loves me – and he who loves me
Will be loved by my Father; and I will love him
And will reveal myself to him."

Judas, not Judas Iscariot, asked him,
"Lord, what is happening that you are to reveal yourself
To us but not to the rest of the world?"
– "If anyone loves me, he will obey my teaching;
My Father will then love him and we will come to him
And make our home with him – not so for the one
Who does not love me and does not obey my teaching.
The words you hear are not mine
But those of the Father who sent me.

"I say this to you while I am with you,
But the Comforter, the Divine Spirit,[1]
Whom the Father will send in my name,
Will teach you all things and remind
You of all the things I told you.
Peace – I leave with you;
Peace – I give you.
I do not give as the world gives.
Do not let your hearts be troubled
And do not be afraid.

"You heard me tell you: I go away but come back to you.
If you love me, you would rejoice that I go to the Father
Because the Father is greater than me.
Now, I have told you this before it happens,
So that when it happens you may still believe.[2]

---

[1] Could St. Paul, whose teaching was that Jesus was more than a physical
Messiah who had come to restore Jewish sovereignty, be the Comforter sent in
Jesus's name, or the one who taught that the faith in Jesus gave the faithful
the gift of the Divine Spirit? There can be no greater comfort than the
knowledge that he whom you have loved and who has died has *not* died but
lives on in you.
[2] If he had not told them, they would lose faith because how could God's
Messiah be killed!

I cannot speak to you much longer
For the earthly ruler is coming.
He has no power over me,
But the world must know that I love the Father
And I must do what the Father has commanded.
Come, let us leave.

15 'Live in me and I will live in you'

"I am the true vine and my Father is the vine keeper.
He removes my branches, which bear no fruit;
He prunes the branches bearing fruit to yield more fruit.
Now, you are pure because of my teaching.
Live in me and I will live in you.
I am the vine and you are the branches.
He who lives in me and I in him will bear much fruit
Because apart from me you achieve nothing.
Anyone who lives not in me is a cut branch that withers;
They are collected to be thrown into the fire and burnt.
If you live in me and my teaching lives in you,
Ask for whatever you require and it shall be.
This glorifies my Father: that, bearing much fruit,
You prove yourselves to be my disciples.

"As the Father has loved me, so have I loved you.
Now, continue to live through my love.
If you meet my demands, you will live through my love;
As I, by obeying my Father's commands, live in his love.
I tell you this that my own rejoicing may be in you
And that your rejoicing will overflow.
This is what I demand: love each other as I have loved you.
There is no greater love than this:
That one lays down his life for his friends.[1]

---

[1] The comfort Jesus offers his disciples for his coming departure is manifold: he
will continue to live in them, his joy will remain in them and they will know
that he has died so that they may be saved.

You are my friends if you do what I demand of you.
No longer do I call you my servants because
The servant cannot question what his master does,
But I have called you friends because everything
My Father has told me, I have shared with you.

"It is not you who chose me, but I who chose you
And sent you to go to bear fruit – lasting fruit –
So that whatever you ask of the Father in my name,
He will give to you; this is what I demand from you:
Love each other.

"If the world hates you, accept that it hated me
Before it hated you; if you are of the world,
It would love you as it loves its own, but it is because
You are not of this world that I have chosen you.
Therefore, the world does hate you.
Remember what I told you:
A servant is not greater than his master.
If they persecuted me, they must also persecute you.[1]
If they obeyed my teaching, they would also obey yours.
But they will act towards you because of me, because
They do not recognise he who has sent me.

"If I had not come and spoken to them,
They would have no guilt;
Now, they have no excuse for their sins.
He who hates me also hates my father.
If I had not performed my works among them,
Which no person ever had, they would not be guilty; but now
They have seen and have hated both me and my Father.
But this is to fulfil what is written in their Law:
They hated me without cause.'[2]

---

[1] St. John has Jesus predicting not St. Paul's persecution of the
Jewish-Christians but the persecution of the Christians in Rome.
[2] *Psalms 35:19; 69:4.* Scholars argue that as St. John is so well versed in the
Scriptures, he was a born Jew. The fact that he describes Psalms as part of

When the Comforter, whom I send from the Father, comes,
The Divine Spirit from the Father will bear witness to me;
But you must also bear witness for me for
You have been with me from the very beginning."[1]

16 'The Comforter will instruct the world He will guide you in the whole truth'

"I have told you this so that you will not be shocked:
They will expel you from the community.
The time will come when all who **seek to** kill you believe
That by doing this, they are **in fact** serving God.
They will do this for they did not know the Father or me.
I tell you this so that when that time does come,
You will remember what I told you;
At the outset, because I was with you,
There was no need for me to tell you this.
Now that I return to the one who sent me,
Not one of you asks, 'Where are you going?'[2]

"Because I tell you this, grief has stricken your hearts.
But I tell you the truth; it is best for you that I go away.
For, if I did not go, the Comforter would not come to you.
But, if I go, I will send him to you; and when he comes,
He will instruct the world in regard to sin, righteousness and
    judgement;
About sin – for you do not believe in me;[3]

---

their Law in an indication that he was not, on two counts: every Jew would
know that Psalms was not part of the Law (Torah) and would call it ours and
not theirs, unless one argues that the biblical quotations were inserted later, in
which case one cannot claim that St. John was steeped in Jewish tradition.
[1] This verse adds to my conviction that the Comforter is St. Paul for it was he
who taught the teaching of Jesus reported by St. John with the added
admonition that the first disciples should also have faith in the divinity of
Christ, and not only in his role as Messiah.
[2] Not true: Thomas asks, see 14:5.
[3] They do not believe that forgiveness from sin can only come through Christ.
St Paul will teach them this.

About righteousness – for you saw me no more when I
    returned to the Father;[1]
About judgement because the Ruler of this world has been
    condemned.[2]

"I have so many more things to tell you,
But you could not bear to hear them now;
But when he of the Divine Spirit comes,
He will guide you in the whole truth.
His words will not come from himself;
He will only say what he hears.
He will declare that which is to come.
That one will glorify me because he will receive
That which is from me and will declare it to you.
All that the Father has is given to me; that is why I say:
He will take what is given to me to declare to you.

"In a little while, you will no longer see me.
But in a little while you will see me again."
Some of the disciples said to each other,
"What does he mean when he tells us:
'In a little while you will not see me but
In a little while you will see me again?'
Also: 'Because I am going to the Father.'"
They kept asking, "What does he mean by 'a little while'?
We do not understand what he is saying."
Jesus knew what they wanted to ask him,
"It is about this that you ask one another because I said,
'In a little while, you will not see me' and then,
'In a little while, you will see me.' In truth I tell you,
You will weep and lament but the world will rejoice.
You will grieve but your grief will turn to joy.

[1] The Comforter would reassure the Christians that the crucifixion of Jesus did not
prove that he was a false Messiah who could not deliver them, but was God's son,
his agent, who was like him, the source of righteousness and repentance.
[2] The death of Jesus was not a defeat but a triumph over Satan, the ruler of
this world. Through the death and resurrection of Christ, God was glorified.

"A woman ready to give birth laments her pain because
Her time has come; but, when she brings forth her child,
She no longer remembers her distress because of her joy
Because a new human being has been born into the world.
So do you now suffer grief but when I see you again,
Your hearts will rejoice – no one will take that joy away.
On that day, you will no longer ask me anything.
In truth I tell you, for whatever you ask in my name,
The Father will give to you;
Until now you have not asked for anything in my name.
Ask and you will receive and your joy will overflow.

"I have spoken to you with figures of speech,
But the time is coming when I will not speak so,
But will speak clearly about the Father.
On that day, you will ask in my name.
I am not saying that I will petition the Father for you:
The Father himself loves you because you loved me
And believed that I came from God.
I came out of the Father and entered the world;
Now I leave the world and go to the Father."

The disciples said, "Now that you speak clearly,
Without images, we understand that you know all things;
You need no one to ask questions of you.
This makes us believe that you have come from God."[1]
Jesus replied, "Do you now believe?
The time is coming, indeed it has come,
That you will disperse each to his own place
And you will leave me all alone but I will not be alone because
the Father is with me.

"I have told you this so that you may find peace through me.
In this world you will suffer distress;
But do take heart; I have conquered the world."

[1] What has persuaded them of this? He has merely told them that he would
answer them clearly at another time.

17 Jesus sees that his time has come
He prays for his disciples

Jesus, after saying this, looking to the heavens, said,
"Father, the time has come:
Glorify your son so that the Son may glorify you;
You gave him authority over all flesh that he might, through
    all that you have given him,
Grant them life eternal; and this is eternal life:
Understanding that you are the only true God   ·
And that he whom you have sent is Jesus Christ.
I have glorified you on earth by completing the work you gave
    me to perform.
Now glorify me Father, through being with you,
With the glory I had with you, before the world began.

"I revealed your essence[1] to those men of the world
You assigned to me[2]; they were yours; you gave them to me.
They have obeyed your teaching; now they understand
That everything you gave me comes from you.
Because I have taught them the teachings you gave to me.
They accepted them, fully aware that I came from you.
They believed that you sent me.[3]

"I ask on their behalf, not on behalf of the world;
But for those you assigned to me, for they are yours.
All that is mine is yours and all that is yours is mine.
And I have been glorified through them.
Now that I am no longer to be in this world,
While they remain in this world, and I return to you,
Holy Father, protect them by the power of your name,

[1] Literally: 'name'.

[2] This does suggest that God had chosen the believers. It is an expression of
Paul's concept of 'grace': the power to have faith in Christ was itself a gift from
God to his chosen ones.

[3] The constant repetition of this theme indicates the questioning and the
overwhelming need to persuade the people that Jesus was sent by God.

Those you gave over to me: let them be one as we are one.[1]
When I was with them, I protected them through the power of
Your name, which you gave to me; and I watched over them;
Not one of them perished except the son of destruction[2]
So that Scripture would be fulfilled.[3]

"I come to you now, but speak these words in this world,
So that they may rejoice in my fulfilment in them.[4]
I have given them your teaching and the world hated them
Because they are not of the world as I am not of the world.[5]
I do not ask that you take them from the world,
But that you keep them away from evil.[6]
They are not of the world as I am not of the world.
By your truth, dedicate them for divine purposes,[7]
For your word is truth; as you sent me into the world,
I also sent them into the world. For them I dedicated myself;
That they also should be dedicated **to you** in truth.

"I not only ask for them but also for those who through
Their words believe in me,[8] that all of them may be as one
As you, Father, are in me and I am in you, that they also
Be in us so that the world will believe that you sent me.

---

[1] This appears to be the confirmation of the unity of the holy community – the Church, which in Paul's letters is the Body of Christ.

[2] This is assumed to be Judas Iscariot; another possible translation: 'destined to be lost'.

[3] The implication is that as Jesus had to be killed, someone had to betray him. See (13:27) where we are told that it is after Judas eats the piece of bread that Jesus gave him, that Satan enters into him.

[4] By his tribute to them as chosen by God and his prayer that God the Father will protect them as he has.

[5] The total identification of the disciples and believers with Jesus is very significant, as a prelude to the Eucharist.

[6] Most translations prefer 'evil one' though the Greek text does not justify it.

[7] The simpler translation: 'sanctify' or 'consecrate' no longer expresses the power of its meaning. In the next two lines 'dedicate' is used in the context of being separated by God to be his agents to achieve his will.

[8] The distinction between the disciples and the believers is significant. It suggests that this gospel was written when the hierarchy in the Church had been established.

I have given to them the glory you gave to me;
That they may be one as we are one:
I in them and you in me; that they are made perfect in one,[1]
So that the world will know that you sent me
And have loved them even as you loved me.
Father, I wish that those you assigned to me were with me,
So that they might witness my glory which you granted
    me
Because you loved me even before the world's creation.
Righteous Father, the world did not know you, but I knew
    you.
And these understand that you sent me;
I made your name known to them, that the love with which
You love me may be theirs as I myself am in them."

18 Jesus is betrayed and arrested
The High Priest and Pilate question him

After these words, Jesus left with his disciples;
He crossed the Kidron Valley;
He and his disciples entered a grove.
Judas, who betrayed him, knew the place, as Jesus had often
    met there with his disciples.
So Judas came with a band of soldiers, some chief priests and
    Pharisees, carrying torches, lamps and weapons.
Jesus, though he knew what was about to happen to him,
Went forward and asked them, "Whom do you seek?"
– "Jesus the Nazarene."
– "I am he."
Judas, who betrayed him, was standing among them.
When Jesus had said, "I am he," they drew back and fell to
    the ground;
Again he asked them, "Whom do you seek?"

---

[1] This teaching of mystical unity is breathtaking and is what gave St. Paul the
power to successfully proselytise among the Gentile communities.

Again they said, "Jesus the Nazarene."
– "I told you that I am he; if you seek me, let them go,"
To fulfil what he had said,
"Of those you gave to me, I lost not any one."
Simon Peter, having a sword, drew it and struck the
High Priest's servant, and cut off his right ear;[1]
The servant's name was Malchus.

Jesus said to Peter, "Put your sword into its sheath.
Must I not drink the cup the Father has given me?"
Thus the band led by its commander and the Jewish guards
took Jesus and bound him.
First, they brought him to Annas;
He was father-in-law to Caiaphas, the incumbent High Priest.
It was Caiaphas who had advised the Jews that it was better
  for one person to die in order to save all the people.[2]

Simon Peter and another disciple, who knew the High Priest,
  followed Jesus.
He entered with Jesus into the High Priest's court;
Peter stayed outside by the door.
The disciple who knew the High Priest had a word with the
  doorkeeper and brought Peter inside;
She asked Peter, "Are you not one of this man's disciples?"
– "I am not."
Because it was cold, a fire was made;
The servants and guards were warming themselves by it.
Peter was also standing with them and warming himself.

The High Priest questioned Jesus about his disciples and
  teachings
Jesus answered him, "I have spoken openly to the world;

[1] The fact that Peter has a sword suggests that he was ready to fight for Jesus
to make him the king of Israel.
[2] The reader should recall his fear that all the Judeans would suffer from a
Roman onslaught if Jesus were recognised as the Messiah – the king of the
Jews. Ironically, it is the Christian faith that he did die for all the Jews, and not
just for them, in order to save humanity from death.

I always taught in the synagogues and in the Temple, where
    Jews come together.
I said nothing in secret. Why do you question me?
Question those who heard what I said;
They know exactly what I said."
As he said this, a guard hit Jesus, saying,
"Is this the way you answer the High Priest?"
– "If I said anything wrong, tell me what;
    But, if I spoke the truth, why did you beat me?"
Annas then sent him bound to Caiaphas, the High Priest.[1]
While Peter was standing and warming himself, they asked
    him,
"Are you not one of his disciples?" He denied it, "I am not."
A relation to the servant whose ear Peter had cut off asked,
"Did I not see you in the grove with him?"
Again, Peter denied it; immediately a rooster crowed.

They brought Jesus from Caiaphas to the Praetorium.[2]
As it was early morning, they did not enter the palace –
To avoid ritual impurity, that they might eat the Passover.[3]
Pilate, therefore, went out to them and asked them,
"What charges are you bringing against this man?"
– "If this man was not doing wrong,
    We would not have brought him to you."
– "Take him yourselves and judge him according to your Law."

---

[1] The lack of historical accuracy is evident not only because this account is in
contradiction to the other gospels, but in the confusion as to who is the High
Priest, Annas or Caiaphas; also the fact that it was very unlikely that the High
Priests would be in session on Passover Eve, after the slaughtering and eating
of the Paschal lamb. It is, however, possible that the Last Supper was not on
Passover Eve, but the night before as is indicated later: 19:14. See fn on p.70,
St. Luke & the Apostles, The People's Bible.

[2] The palace of the Roman governor.

[3] The Paschal lamb, but this would have been eaten on the eve, unless it is
referring to the festival sacrifice. But, why should entering the palace defile
them? It seems to be a further attempt to show the Jews in a bad light; they
are prepared to conspire to kill the Son of God, but are concerned about their
ritual purity!

– "It is not within our authority to execute anyone."
This was so the word of Jesus should be fulfilled when
He indicated the manner of his death.

So Pilate went into his palace and summoned Jesus.
He asked him "Are you king of the Jews?"
– "Is this what you think or were you told this about me?"
– "I am not a Jew **who cares about this**;
   Your nation and your chief priests handed you over to me.
   What is it that you have done?"
– "My kingdom is not of this world;
   If my kingdom were of this world,
   My supporters would have fought to prevent my arrest
   by the Jews but my kingdom is not here."[1]
– "So then you are a king?"
– "It is you who say that I am a king,
   I have been born for this and
   For this I have come into the world –
   To give witness to the truth;
   Everyone who is part of the truth
   Hears my voice."
"What is truth!" was Pilate's response.[2]
After this, he went out to the Jews and told them,
"I find him guilty of no crime,
But as it is your custom for me to pardon one prisoner at the
   Passover.
Do you wish me to release to you the king of the Jews?"[3]

---

[1] Were he the Messiah, he would have allowed Peter to defend him In *St. Luke*,
23:3, Jesus does not deny he is King of the Jews. In reply to the question, he
says, "You say so."

[2] By denying that he was the Messiah, in the sense of a king sent to restore
Jewish independence, he was not guilty of sedition. When Jesus speaks of the
truth, Pilate loses interest; his question is asked with disdain, indicated by the
fact that he is not interested in the answer.

[3] This is a most extraordinary and self-contradictory account. If Pilate finds that
Jesus is not guilty of sedition as he says that he is not an earthly king, he
should just release him. There is no reason for the people to ask for it. There is
also no justification for him referring to Jesus as king of the Jews. If the

They cried out again,[1] "Not this man, but Barabbas."
This Barabbas was a robber.

19 Jesus is crucified as King of the Jews

[2]Pilate then took Jesus and had him flogged;
The soldiers, having plaited a wreath of thorns,
Put it on his head; they threw a purple cloth on him.
They then surrounded him shouting,
"Hail, King of the Jews!"
They battered him with blows. Pilate went out again:
"Look, I am bringing him out to you,
So that you know that I find him guilty of no crime."[3]
Jesus appeared: the wreath of thorns and purple robe on him.
Pilate said to them, "Here is the man."

When they saw him, the chief priests[4] and guards shouted,
"Crucify, crucify!" Pilate replied, "Then crucify him for
I can find no crime of which he is guilty." The Jews said,

---

narrative is consistent, now that Caiaphas is satisfied that the messianic claims
for Jesus would not bring the weight of Roman power down on the nation, he
would have no reason to wish his execution. So Pilate is playing with the Jews,
and has taken the matter out of the hands of the High Priest.

[1] They had not cried out before. One needs to ask how a large crowd came to
assemble.

[2] What follows is an extraordinary fabrication – the consequence of the
confusion of two accusations against Jesus: 1) the claim that he is the
Anointed One, the King of the Jews, and therefore a rebel against Rome; 2)
the claim that he is the Son of God and therefore a blasphemer against the
Jewish Faith. When Pilate finds no crime in him, as he denies the former, he
should neither have him flogged nor allow him to be scorned as a king by his
soldiers. The portrayal of the ruthless Roman Governor as an innocent
bystander was motivated by the desire to heap calumny upon the Jews for his
divinely ordained death.

[3] As Jesus is about to appear dressed as a king, were this account factual, they
could not have believed in Pilate's sincerity when they saw a bruised and
beaten Jesus hauled before them, crowned in a wreath of thorns. Perhaps,
Pilate was trying to trick them into acknowledging Jesus as their king.

[4] It is unlikely that the leading priests would demean themselves in such mob
frenzy.

"We have a Law and, according to the Law, he must die,
Because he has claimed to be the Son of God."[1]
When Pilate heard this, he was frightened and went inside.[2]
"Where do you come from?" he asked Jesus,
But Jesus gave him no answer.
– "Will you not speak to me?
   Are you not aware that I have the power to release you
   and the power to crucify you?"
– "You have no power over me except that which was given
      to you from above;
   Therefore, the one who handed me over to you is more
      sinful."[3]

Because of this, Pilate attempted to release him;[4]
But the Jews shouted, "If you release this man,
You are no friend of Caesar, for anyone
Who claims to be king rebels against Caesar."[5]
Hearing this, Pilate brought Jesus outside;

[1] The fact is that there is no such law, because such a claim was unheard of when the Torah was codified and indeed in the time when Jesus lived. The gospels indicate their awareness of this by the fact that the apostles cannot comprehend the concept of a Son of God sent to die to achieve atonement for human sin and eternal life for those who believed in him. This is why the Comforter, St Paul, has to come, in order to explain this totally un-Jewish concept. The irony is that, had Jesus made such a claim, he, with all his miracles, could not persuade the Jews, nor could his disciples. Only St. Paul succeeded, but that was because his mission was to the Gentiles, who, due to the influence of the prevailing mystery religions and the deification of the Roman Emperors, were more susceptible to his persuasive powers than were the Jews – at least those who had not acculturated themselves to Hellenistic life and thought.

[2] What was he frightened of, that he was the Son of God? Pilate, as a Roman, could more easily relate to such a claim, than that a Jew could hope to defeat the Roman Empire.

[3] The logic here escapes me – a transparent attempt to shift responsibility from the Romans to the Jews?

[4] As he has just claimed he had the power to do so, there was nothing to prevent him.

[5] But he did not claim to be king; Pilate could have told them this. Also, in contradiction to this, Pilate was previously told that Jesus must die because he claimed to be the Son of God, not the Messiah.

He sat down on the seat of judgement in the place known as
The Stone Pavement, which in Aramaic is Gabbatha.
Now, it was the day for preparing the Passover.
At noon, he said to the Jews, "Here is your king!"[1]
– "Crucify him!"
– "Shall I crucify your king?"
– "We have no king but Caesar!"[2]
So he delivered him to them[3] to be crucified.[4]
So they took Jesus; carrying his own cross,
He went to Golgotha, meaning in Aramaic
The Place of the Skull, where he was to be crucified.
There were two others with him, one on either side;
Jesus was in the middle.

Pilate had a sign written and fastened on the cross:
JESUS THE NAZOREAN[5] THE KING OF THE JEWS.
Many Jews saw this sign because there was a town
Near to the place of Jesus's crucifixion;
Also, the sign was written in Aramaic, Latin and Greek.
The chief priests of the Jews protested to Pilate,
"It should not say 'The King of the Jews' but that
'This man claimed to be King of the Jews.'"
Pilate dismissed them, "What I have written is written."[6]

---

[1] This mocking statement to the Jews is inexplicable, as Pilate has heard Jesus
deny the claim and the Jews wanting his death on the basis of the claim. In
spite of the narrator's political agenda, he is too honest to conceal Pilate's
mischievous and ruthless nature.

[2] Pilate's question seems to compel the Jews to make this answer if they are to
avoid being classed as rebels against Rome.

[3] It will soon become apparent that 'them' can only refer to the Roman
soldiers.

[4] This entire sequence contradicts the statement that he attempted to release
him.

[5] Nazorean is a closer approximation to the Greek text than Nazarene, which is
used by most translations. The accepted meaning is 'of Nazareth'. For a fuller
comment see fn p. 84, *St. Luke & The Apostles, The People's Bible.*

[6] The sign is a warning from Pilate that crucifixion is the fate of those who
claim to be a king of the Jews.

When the soldiers crucified Jesus, they took his clothes;
They divided them into four shares, one for each of them.
The tunic remained; it was without seams, one woven piece.
They said, "Let us not tear it; let us draw lots for it."
This happened to fulfil Scriptures:
"They divided my clothing among themselves;
And drew lots for my clothing."[1]
And this is what the soldiers did.

By the cross of Jesus stood his mother, his mother's sister,
Mary, the wife of Clopas and Mary of Magdala.
Jesus, seeing his mother there and the disciple he loved,
He said to his mother, "He will be a son to you,"
And to the disciple, "She will be a mother to you."[2]
From that time, the disciple had her live in his home.
Once he knew that everything had been done so that
the Scriptures might be fulfilled,
Jesus said, "I am thirsty."[3]
A jar, full of vinegar being there,
A sponge was soaked in it, stuck to a hyssop branch and raised
    to Jesus's lips.
On receiving the vinegar, Jesus said, "It is fulfilled."
He inclined his head and surrendered his spirit.

The Jews, as it was the day of preparation **for the Passover**,
Did not want bodies remaining on the crosses on the Sabbath.[4]
Especially, as the next day was so important a Sabbath,
They asked Pilate to have their legs broken and taken down.[5]

---

[1] *Psalms, 22:18*
[2] Jesus offers poignant comfort. As he loved them both and was loved by them, they will experience this love through each other.
[3] *Psalms 69:21*: the suffering servant is given vinegar to quench his thirst.
[4] In the Hebrew Bible, days of holy convocation are often referred to as Sabbaths because they were, as the seventh day Sabbath, days of rest. Jewish law also insisted on immediate burial as a sign of respect.
[5] From what follows it would seem that they are seeking to hasten their deaths by causing them to bleed to death through the rupture – cruel but in some sense merciful, as crucifixion was a horrible way to die.

The soldiers came and broke the legs of the first man
And the other man who were crucified with Jesus.
When they came to Jesus, they saw that he was dead,
They did not break his legs, but one of the soldiers pierced

Jesus's side with a lance; blood and water came out.
The man who saw this gave testimony, which is true;
Knowingly, he tells the truth so that you too might believe.[1]
These things happened to fulfil Scriptures:
"Not one of his bones shall be broken."[2]
And elsewhere in Scriptures,
"They shall look at him whom they pierced."[3]

Later, Joseph of Arimathea, secretly a disciple of Jesus,
Out of his fear of the Jews, asked Pilate for Jesus's body.
Pilate assented; he came and took his body.
Nicodemus, the one who had earlier visited Jesus by night,
Went with him, bearing a mixture of myrrh and aloes,
Weighing more than half a hundredweight.
They took the body of Jesus and wrapped it with the spices, in
    cloths of linen in accordance with Jewish burial rites.
Now, in the place of his crucifixion, there was a garden;
In the garden there was a new tomb, in which no one had
    ever been put to rest.
Because of the preparation of the Jews **for the Passover,**
And as the tomb was nearby, they laid Jesus there.

[1] In addition to proving what follows, it may have been to prove that he had actually died and was not brought down alive from the cross – this would explain his resurrection to the sceptics.

[2] This is a commandment concerning the Paschal lamb with which Jesus is here identified; he is also compared to an innocent lamb elsewhere in *St. John*; also in *Acts* 8:32 and *1 Peter*1: 19. It may be that they never broke the legs of those on crucifixes, but told the tale as a pretext for explaining why Jesus's legs were not broken.

[3] *Zechariah* 12:10. The prophesy of Zechariah is filled with Messianic hopes.

20 The resurrection of Jesus
He appears to his disciples

On the first day of the week,
Mary of Magdala came early,
It still being dark, to the tomb;
She saw that the rock had been removed from the tomb.
She ran to Simon Peter and to the other disciple –
The one whom Jesus loved; she said to them,
"They took the Lord out of the tomb and
We do not know where they have put him."
Peter and the other disciple rushed to the tomb.
Both were running together,
But as the other disciple ran more quickly than Peter,
He reached the tomb first, and looking in,
Saw the linen cloths but did not go in.
Simon Peter, arriving after him, went into the tomb.
He saw the linen cloths lying there and the kerchief that had
    been around Jesus's head.
It was folded up in a place away from the linen cloths.
The other disciple who had first reached the tomb went in.
When he saw **that the body was gone**, he believed.
(They still did not understand from Scriptures that
He had to rise from the dead.)[1]
The disciples returned to their homes,
But Mary stood outside the tomb weeping.
As she wept, she stooped into the tomb,
She saw two angels dressed in white sitting where the
body of Jesus had been:
One at the place of his head;
The other at the place of his feet.
They asked her, "Woman, why do you weep?"

---

[1] The parenthetical note is confirming that until the disappearance of his body, the disciples did not understand (*St. Luke* 18:34) when Jesus told them that he was to die and be raised from the dead. St. Matthew also records Jesus's declaration but not their lack of understanding of its meaning.

– "They have taken my Lord
  And I do not know where they have put him."[1]

Saying this, she turned away and saw Jesus standing there;
She did not realize that it was Jesus. He asked her,
"Woman, why are you weeping; for whom are you looking?"
Thinking that he was the gardener, she answered him,
"Sir, if you were the one who removed him,
Tell me where you put him and I will get him."
Jesus said to her, "Mary."
Turning to him, she exclaimed, "Rabboni!"(meaning teacher)
Jesus said, "Do not touch me,
For I have not gone up to the Father.
Go to my brothers and tell them,
'I am going up to my father and your father,
And to my God and your God.'"

Mary of Magdala went to the disciples with the news that
She had seen the Lord and what he had said to her.
It was in the early evening of the first day of the week;
The doors had been firmly shut where the disciples stayed
Because of their fear of the Jews.
Jesus came and stood among them; he said,
"Peace to you." After saying this, he showed them
His **pierced** hands and his **pierced** side.
The disciples rejoiced at seeing the Lord.
Again Jesus said to them, "Peace to you.
As the Father sent me, so do I send you."
After saying this he breathed into them, saying,
"Receive the Divine Spirit,
Whatever sins you have forgiven; they are forgiven.
If you hold back forgiveness, it is withheld."

Now Thomas, called Didymus, one of the Twelve
Was not with them when Jesus came.

---

[1] This would suggest that the disciples still did not believe in the Resurrection
or, if they did, did not bother to reassure Mary of their belief

When the other disciples said to him,
"We have seen the Lord," he exclaimed,
"Unless I see the nail marks on his hands
And put my fingers where the nails were
And put my hand into his side **where he was pierced**
I will not believe it." Eight days later,
The disciples were again in the same house and Thomas was
    with them.
The doors were firmly shut, yet Jesus came and stood among
    them saying, "Peace be to you."
Then he says to Thomas, "Bring your finger here;
See my hands; take your hand and put it into my side.
Stop doubting and believe."

Thomas replied to him, "My Lord and my God."
Jesus said, "Since you have seen me, now do you believe?
Blessed are those who have not seen and yet believe."[1]
Jesus performed many more signs before his disciples,
Which have not been recorded in this book,
But these have been recorded that you may believe that
Jesus is the Messiah, the Son of God, and that by believing
You may have life **eternal** in his name.

21 Jesus appears on the shore of Tiberius
He teaches his disciples how to fish

After these events, Jesus appeared again to his disciples by the
    Sea of Tiberius; this is how he appeared:
Simon Peter, Thomas, called Didymus,

---

[1] Objectively, one needs to comment that the disciples are not less faithless then
the 'Jews'. Had they seen his reappearance and his performance of miracles,
would they not also have believed? The fact is that nowhere in Jewish
Scriptures was there the promise of one individual dying and being resurrected.
If Thomas the disciple will not believe without visible proof, it is an
extraordinary demand to make of those who never saw the living Jesus before
his death. It is a leap of faith which can only be made on the authority of
tradition.

Nathaniel from Cana in Galilee,
The sons of Zebedee and two other disciples were together.
Simon Peter told them, "I am going fishing."
They said, "We will go with you."
They went and boarded the boat;
During that night they caught nothing.
Early in the morning, Jesus was standing on the shore.
The disciples did not know that it was Jesus.
He called out, "Children, have you not caught any fish."
"No," came back their reply. So he instructed them,
"Cast your nets on the right side of the boat and
You will find some." When they did, they could not haul in
The net because there were so many fish.

The disciple whom Jesus loved said to Peter,
"It is the Lord." When Peter heard that it was the Lord,
Being naked, he put his clothes on and threw himself into the sea;
The other disciples followed in the small boat,
Towing the net full of fish, to the shore which was not far
    away – some hundred yards.
When they landed they saw a coal fire with fish and bread on it.
Jesus said, "Bring some of the fish you have caught."
Simon Peter went and hauled the net to the shore;
It was full with a hundred and fifty-three fish,
Remarkably, with so many fish, the net was not torn.
Jesus said to them, "Come and have breakfast."
No one dared to question him, "Who are you?"
They felt sure that it was the Lord.
Jesus approached, took the bread and gave it to them;
He did this with the fish as well.

Now, this was the third time that Jesus appeared to
The disciples after he was raised from the dead.
When they finished eating, Jesus said to Simon Peter,
"Simon son of John, do you love me more than these?"
– "Yes, Lord, you know that I love you."
– "Feed my lambs."

Again, Jesus said to Simon son of John,
"Simon son of John, do you love me?"
– "Yes, Lord, you know that I love you."
– "Be a shepherd for my little sheep."
A third time, he said to him,
"Simon son of John, do you love me?"
Peter was upset when for a third time Jesus had asked him,
"Do you love me?"
– "Lord, you know all things; you know that I love you."
– "Feed my little sheep.
In truth I tell you, when you were younger,
You dressed yourself and went wherever you desired;
When you grow old, you will stretch out your hands and
Another will dress you and take you
Where you have no desire to go."

He said this to indicate with what death he would glorify God.
After saying this, he said, "Follow me."
When he looked back, Peter saw the disciple whom Jesus loved
following him –
The one who at the supper had leaned against him, who said,
"Lord, who is going to betray you?" Seeing him, Peter asked,
"Lord, what about him?"
– "If I want him to remain alive until my return,
What is that to you, you must follow me."
For this reason a rumour spread among the brothers that that
disciple would not die;
But Jesus had not said to him that he would not die;
He only said, "If I wish him to remain alive until my return,
what is it to you?"

This is the disciple who witnessed these things
And who recorded these things and we know that he is a
truthful witness.
But there are many other things which Jesus did;
Were they all recorded, I do not think that the world
Would be big enough to contain all those books.

THE LETTERS OF ST. JOHN

The First Letter

1 *The Word which gives life is our theme*

That which was at the beginning, which we have heard[1],
And that which we have seen with our eyes,
What we looked on and touched[2] – the Word, which gives life.
This is our theme: that life was made visible.
We saw and bear witness and proclaim to you the eternal life
    which was with the Father[3] but became visible to us.
We proclaim to you what we have seen and what we have
    heard so that you may join us in fellowship –
Iindeed our fellowship which is with the Father and with his
    son, Jesus Christ.
We write this so that our joy may be complete.

This is the message we received from him and transmit to you:
God is light; there is no darkness in him.
Were we to say that we are in fellowship with him,
Yet walk in darkness, we lie and do not live truthfully.
But, if we walk in light as he is in the light,
We are in fellowship with each other;
The blood of Jesus, his son cleanses us from all sin.
If we say that we are without sin, we deceive ourselves and
    there is no truth in us;
If we own up to our sins, he is true and just and will forgive
    our sins and cleanse us of all iniquity.
If we say that we have not sinned,
We are calling him a liar and his word is not in us.

---

[1] Is this referring to the story of creation in *Genesis?*
[2] The disciples were witness to the life, death and resurrection of Jesus.
[3] Previously, only God was immortal. Through Jesus, all believers can become immortal by participating in his resurrection.

2 *The antichrist denies the Father and Son*

My little children, I write to you to exhort you not to sin.
But, if anyone does sin, we have an advocate with the
    Father:
Jesus Christ, the righteous one.
He is the atonement for our sins,
And not just ours, but of the entire world.[1]
We prove that we know him if we keep his commandments.
He who says he knows him but does not keep his command is
    a liar and there is no truth in the man.
However, whoever lives by his word,
He will truly be fulfilled with God's love in him.
By this, we know that we are in him.
He, who says he is in him,
Must walk in the way that Jesus walked.

Beloved, I am not writing you a new command
But an old command that you had at the beginning;
The old command is the word you have heard.
Yet there is a new command that I am writing to you:
That is true in his life and true in your life
Because the darkness is passing
And the true light is shining already.
Anyone who says that he lives in the light
But hates his brother still lives in darkness.
One who loves his brother lives in the light
And there is no fault in him.
The one who hates his brother lives and walks in darkness;
He knows not where he goes because the darkness has blinded
    him.

---

[1] Jesus is the sacrificial atonement not only for the sins of Israel, but for all
humanity. This was the decisive difference between the apostles, Peter and
Paul, the former seeing Jesus as the redeemer of Israel and the latter as the
redeemer of all humankind

I write to you, little children,[1]
  because your sins have been forgiven through his name.[2]
I write to you, fathers,[3]
  because you have known him[4] from the beginning.
I write to you, young men
  because you have overcome the evil one.[5]
I write to you, little children
  because you have known the Father.[6]
I write to you, fathers
  because you have known him from the beginning.
I write to you, young men
  because you are strong and the word of God lives in you.
You have overcome the evil one.

Do not love the world; do not love worldly things.
The love of the Father is not in anyone who loves the world.[7]
For everything in the world: the lust of the flesh,
The lust of the eyes and the vanities of life come not from the
  Father but is of the world.
The world and its lust is passing away,
But he who obeys the will of God will live forever.[8]
Young children, this is the final hour.

---

[1] Recent believers, i.e. 'infants in Christ', *1 Corinthians* 3:1
[2] In the Bible, the name reveals the essence of the personality, whether the person is a human or God.
[3] The early believers.
[4] Jesus.
[5] In Judaism, he would have been called 'the evil inclination', the libido that becomes active in adolescence.
[6] Novices in the faith would have previously believed in 'God the Father'.
[7] This is a very different message from that of Judaism, which is to enjoy life to the full within the parameter of permitted behaviour. The diversion from this approach is based on St. Paul's belief in the impending advent in his own lifetime of the Kingdom of God, judgement day, and the resurrection of the dead. In his letters, he recommends against any distractions, which would tie a person down, such as marriage. See *1 Corinthians, ch. 7*, preferably in *The People's Bible: The Genius of Paul (his letters)*.
[8] This is further confirmation of the Pauline view that the end of days was soon to come.

As you have heard, the antichrist is **still** coming.

Already many antichrists have reared their heads.

They came from us but were not us for if they belonged with
us, they would have stayed with us.

This proves that they should never have been part of us.[1]

But it is you, who have been anointed through the Holy One,

And you know the whole truth.

I am writing to you not because you do not know the truth,

But because you do, and no lie comes out of the truth.

Who is the liar if not he who denies Jesus as the Christ?[2]

This is the antichrist: he who denies the Father and Son.[3]

Everyone denying the Son cannot have the Father.

He who confesses faith in the Son has the Father.

Let what you learnt at the beginning remain in you.

If you hold firm to what you heard in the beginning,

You will remain both in the Son and the Father.

This is what he promised us **for so doing** – life eternal.[4]

I am writing this to you about those who seek to mislead you.

As for you, the anointing you received from him lives in you;

You need no further teaching from anyone.

Being anointed through him teaches you about all things.

As it is true and not false, live in him as he taught you.

Now, little children, continue to live in him,

So that when he reappears, we may be self-confident and not
be ashamed before him.

---

[1] This is circuitous reasoning, but what is significant is the revelation that the antichrists were themselves Christians, those 'false apostles' whom St. Paul compares to 'Satan masquerading as a messenger of light'. See *11 Corinthians 11:13–14*. They believed that Jesus was the Messiah but not the Son of God – God incarnate. They certainly were not the Jews who were not in the frame at all as they rejected Jesus even as a purely human messiah.

[2] Christ which is the Greek for Messiah, anointed one, here takes on the new meaning: God made into flesh, as is apparent from the next verse.

[3] The Son is as much God as is the Father.

[4] What was heard from the beginning in Judea was that Jesus was the Messiah, not God made in the flesh. But this was the essence of the message delivered by St. Paul to the gentile communities.

If you believe that he is righteous,
You know that everyone who is righteous is born of him.[1]

3 *Those born of God cannot sin*

Consider the grandeur of the love the Father has given us –
That we should be called the children of God, which we are!
The world does not accept us because it did not accept him.
Beloved, now that we are children of God,
What we are to be has not yet been made known.
But we know that, when he appears, we will be like him,
Because we will see him as he really is.
Everyone who has this hope in him is purified, as he is pure.
Whoever sins, breaks the law for sin is lawlessness.
You know that he came to bear our sins,
Though there is no sin in him.
Whoever lives in him does not sin.
Those who sin have neither seen nor acknowledged him.[2]

Little children, let no one mislead you:
Those who act righteously are righteous as he is righteous.
The sinful belong to the devil since the devil was sinful from
    the very beginning.
For this reason the Son of God appeared to undo the works of
    the devil.
No one born of God sins because his seed lives in him.
Indeed, he cannot sin because he has been born of God![3]

[1] What is being taught here is total identity with God through the Son. This faith grants righteousness and eternal life. St. John continues and perhaps develops the message of St. Paul.

[2] This is the mystical concept of the power of faith in Christ: the believer, as part of Christ, cannot sin for there is no sin in Christ.

[3] As Jesus is the 'seed' of God and as those who believe in him become God's children through him, they cannot sin just as Jesus cannot sin. This is an interesting resolution of the faith vs. acts dilemma. Faith in Christ makes the faithful part of Christ and therefore incapable of evil. A wicked Christian cannot, therefore, be a true believer for faith leads to righteousness. This is in essence St. Paul's teaching: being in Christ means that the Law becomes superfluous for gods need no laws.

This is how it is known who are the children of God and who
    are the children of the devil.
Anyone who does not do what is right is not of God –
Nor is anyone who does not love his brother.

This is the message we heard at the beginning:
We should love one another – not like Cain who came from
    the Evil One[1] and murdered his brother.
And for what reason did he murder him?
Because his own actions were evil
But the actions of his brother were righteous.[2]
Brothers, are you surprised if the world hates you?
We know that we have moved from death to life because we
    love our brothers.
He who does not love his brother – his life is a living death.[3]
He who hates his brother is a murderer.
And you know that no murderer has eternal life in him.

By this we know the meaning of love:
He laid down his life for us;
So ought we to lay down our lives for our brothers.
If a person of means sees his brother in need and shuts himself
    off from him,
How can the love of God be in him?
Little children, let our love not be mere lip service
But in true acts **of righteousness and compassion.**
By this we shall know that we are since**rely in Christ.**[4]
And, when we are in his presence, we can be confident even if
    our conscience makes us feel guilty,
For God, who knows all things is greater than our conscience.

[1] Satan.

[2] This is a tautology that explains nothing.

[3] Literally, 'remains in death'.

[4] This line and the next three are obscure. Where I translate: 'sincerely in
Christ', the literal text is 'in truth'. The intent of the passage seems to be that,
if they behave well because they have faith in Christ, their consciences need
not disturb them, for even the righteous feel guilty, as God will recognise them
as his children and forgive them.

Beloved, if our consciences do not condemn us,
We will be confident before God.
Whatever our petition, he will grant it because we have been
   obedient to his commandment and what we do pleases him.
This is his commandment: believe in the name of his son,
Jesus Christ and love one another, as he commanded us.
He who keeps his commandments lives in him and he in
   him.
By this, we know that he lives in us –
Through the **divine** spirit he has granted us.

4 *God is love – he who lives in love lives in God*

Beloved, do not believe in every spiritual teaching.
Test them to decide whether they come from God because false
   prophets abound in the world.
By this you will recognise the spirit of God:
Every spiritual teaching which confirms that Jesus Christ has
   come in the human flesh is from God.
Every spiritual teaching rejecting Jesus **as coming in the flesh** is
   not from God.
This is the spirit of the antichrist who you heard was coming
   and is now already in the world.

Little children, you are from God; you have overcome them,
Because greater is the one in you[1] than the one in the world.[2]
They are of this world; therefore they speak in worldly terms
   and the world listens to them.
We are from God, so only those knowing God listen to us.
He who is not from God does not listen to us.
Through this we know what is spiritual truth and what is a
   spiritual falsehood.

[1] Jesus, God incarnate.
[2] 'The one in the world' is the antichrist. The antichrist is the Jewish Christian
who affirms the resurrection of Jesus and waits his return as Messiah-King. In
this context, being of this world signifies their incomprehension that God could
have a human son. St. John now develops this theme.

Beloved, let us love one another because love is divine.[1]
Everyone who loves has been born of God and knows God.
Whoever loves not does not know God because God is love.
This is how God revealed his love for us because God sent
   his only begotten son into the world that
   we might live through him.
This is love:
Not that we have loved God but that he loved us and sent his
   son as an atonement for our sins.   ·
Beloved, if God loves us so much, we must love one another.
No one has ever seen God.
If we love one another God lives in us and his love is fulfilled
   in us.

By this, we know that we live in him and he in us because of
   his spirit which he granted to us;
We bear witness that the Father has sent the Son as Saviour of
   the world.
Anyone who affirms that Jesus is the Son of God,
God lives in him and he lives in God.
We know and believe the love that God has for us.
God is love and he who lives in love lives in God and God lives
   in him.
By this has love been fulfilled in us –
To give us confidence in the Day of Judgement because
   in this world we are as he was.
There is no fear in love for fulfilled love drives out fear.[2]
Fear is due to the anticipation of punishment.
The one who is in fear has not been fulfilled in his love.

We love because he first loved us.
Anyone who says "I love God" and hates his brother is a liar.
For anyone who does not love his brother whom he has seen,
   cannot love god whom he has not seen.

---

[1] This panegyric on love seems inspired by St. Paul: *1 Corinthians ch.13.*
[2] The believer knows that he has no reason to fear punishment

This is the commandment we have from him:
In order to love God, one must love his brother.

5 *Whoever has the Son has life*

Everyone who believes that Jesus is the Christ born of God
And everyone who loves the Father loves his begotten one.
So we know that we love the children of God whenever
We love God and obey his commandments.
This is how we love God: by keeping his commandments.
His commandments are not burdensome because everyone
   begotten of God conquers the world.[1]

This is the victory – our faith has conquered the world!
Who can conquer the world except those who believe that
   Jesus is the Son of God[2]?
This is the one who came through water and blood[3] –
Jesus Christ, not only water, but also by blood and water.
It is the **divine** spirit that bears witness
And the **divine** spirit is truth.[4] Three bear witness:
The **divine** spirit, the water[5] and the blood.[6]

---

[1] The complete identification of the believers with Christ should be noted. The evils of the world can be resisted if one, like Christ, is the child of God.

[2] It cannot be repeated enough that this declaration is directed to 'dissidents' within the 'holy community' who did not accept that Jesus was God incarnate. Faith in this principle is required to make the believer part of God through Christ. Without this faith one does not acquire the gift of the divine spirit, which bestows eternal life.

[3] Water refers to the baptism introduced by John the Baptiser, which St. Paul refers to as the baptism of repentance. Blood refers to the baptism of the divine spirit, which comes from faith that God sacrificed Jesus, his only begotten son, to atone for all human sins. This doctrine led to the introduction of the Eucharist as the ritual of redemption: Jesus says, 'Unless you eat the flesh of the Son of Man and drink his blood you have no life in yourselves.' *St. John 6:53*

[4] God is love but God is also truth.

[5] This refers to John the Baptiser's affirmation of Jesus whom he baptised. John says, 'I baptise with water . . .' *St John1: 26*, and, 'Look, there is the lamb of God'(1: 36)

[6] Jesus bears witness to this. See p. 16 fn. 1.

The three bear witness with one voice.
If we are prepared to accept the testimony of men,
Surely, the testimony from God is more significant
Because he is God! He has testified about his only son.

Whoever believes in the Son of God has the witness in him.[1]
Anyone who does not believe God is calling God a liar since
He does not believe in God's testimony about his son.
This is the testimony: God gave us eternal life
And this life is in his son **and is ours through him.**
Whoever has the Son has life.
Whoever does not have the son does not have life.
I write these things that you who believe in the name of
The Son of God may know that you have eternal life.

We are confident that whatever we ask of him,
He will grant us if it accords with his plan
And, if we know that whatever we ask he grants us,
We know that we already possess that which we asked of him.

If one sees his brother committing a deadly sin,
He should pray and he will grant him life –
That is only for those whose sins are not deadly.
I am not speaking about praying for mortal sinners.
All wrongdoing is sinful but not all sins lead to death.
We know that those born of God do not sin –
He who was begotten by God watches over him and the Evil
    One cannot touch him.
We know that we are of God but the entire world is subjected
    to the Evil One.
We know that the Son of God has come and has granted us
    the understanding to know the true one;
And we live in the true one – in his son, Jesus Christ.
This is the true God and **the source of** eternal life.
Little children, be wary of false gods.

---

[1] This is the divine spirit which enters the faithful.

The Second Letter

From the Elder

To the chosen[1] lady and her children,

Whom I sincerely love, and not only I but all who
   know the truth because the truth lives
   in us and will be with us forever.

Grace, mercy and peace from the Father

And from Jesus Christ, the Son of the Father, will be with us in
   love and truth.

I rejoiced exceedingly to find that some of your children walked
   in truth,

By the commandment we had from the Father.

Now, dear lady, I ask you to understand that I am not writing

A new commandment[2], but one we had from the beginning:

That we should love one another and this is love –

To walk according to his commandments.

You heard the commandment from the very beginning. on the
   path you were to follow.

But many deceivers went out into the world –

Those who did not believe that Jesus Christ came in the flesh.

Such a person is the deceiver and the antichrist.[3]

Watch yourselves, lest all your work be lost;

Accept the truth so that you may be rewarded fully.

Anyone who goes ahead not in the teaching of Christ does not
   have God **in him;**

He who is loyal to the teaching has both the Father and the Son.

---

[1] The word might suggest 'election' i.e. members of a holy community
(Church).

[2] This continual protest of St. John that his message of God incarnate is not
knew would seem to indicate that at least for many it was.

[3] Whatever perception was later to develop on the identity of the antichrist,
there can be no doubt that for St. John, he was the spirit of those Christians
who rejected Christ as God born into the flesh. St. Peter, St. Thomas and all of
Jesus's disciples, for whom such a concept would have been utterly foreign,
ironically would have themselves held this heresy.

If anyone comes to you without bringing this teaching,
Do not receive him into your home or even greet him.
Whoever greets him participates in his evil doings.

I have much to write to you about but do not propose to use
    pen and paper;
But my hope is to be with you to talk to you face to face, so
    that our joy may be complete.
The children of your chosen sister[1] send their greetings.

The Third Letter

From the Elder
To my beloved friend Gaius whom I love in truth.
Beloved, I pray that you prosper and enjoy good health just as
    your soul is prospering.
I rejoiced exceedingly when some brothers came to me and told
    me about your loyalty and how you walk in the way of the
    truth.
There is no greater joy for me than to hear that my children
    are walking in the way of the truth.

Beloved, faithful has been your work for the brothers,
Even when they were strangers to you.
They have testified to your love before the Church.
You do well to help them on their way, as God would
    approve.
For the sake of the Name they set out, taking nothing from the
    heathen.
We, therefore, must cultivate such men
So that we may become co-workers for the truth.

I wrote of certain matters to the members of the Church,
But, Diotrephes, who preens himself as its foremost member
    will have nothing of us;

---

[1] Perhaps, members of a sister community.

Therefore, when I come, I will remind him of his doings, his
   malicious words about us.
Not satisfied with this, he does not welcome our brothers.
He prevents those who would like to welcome them.
Indeed, he expels them from the Church!
Beloved, do not follow the bad example, but the good one.
Whoever does good is of God; the evil doer has not seen him.
Demetrius is well spoken of by all – even by truth itself.
We also vouch for him and you know the truth of our views.
I have much to write to you about but not with pen and ink.
I hope to see you very soon when we can talk face to face.

Peace to you.
The friends here send their greetings.
Greet the friends there by name.

The Revelation of
St. John

Introduction

When it was decided to begin publishing the new translation with a taster of three volumes from the Old Testament and one from the New Testament, I winced when Christopher Sinclair-Stevenson suggested that the latter should be *Revelation* because it would create a lot of interest. A cursory reading of it as a young student of the Bible made me cringe. The panoply of monsters under the command of Satan fighting a battle to the death against angels led by the Lamb Jesus gave me no pleasure, as its outcome was the destruction of the goodies with the baddies, indeed of the whole world. I was reassured that it was not just Jewish prejudice because I heard that it was also an embarrassment to many good Christians. It also read like gibberish. The irony is the fact that it was its very incomprehensibility that make people want to read and understand it. There is nothing more fascinating to a reader than a mystery which requires unravelling, and when he is taken along the trail of its solution by the author. In the case of *Revelation*, this would be the task of the translator. I dreaded this challenge, as I was afraid that it was beyond my talents. As it was the last book of the Bible, I could justify my cowardice in putting off the evil day.

How explain, therefore, when I am less than halfway through my translations that I have taken on this fearsome task? My perception of the development of Christianity from a Jewish sect to a religion capable of conquering the world through translating *St. Luke*, *The Acts of the Apostles* and *The Letters of Paul* made me want to skip the other two synoptic gospels, *St. Matthew* and *St. Mark* to take on the theological *St. John*. While translating it, I felt that he, like Paul, had the rare ability to combine theology with poetry. During its translation, my sense that he was speaking of Jesus bringing the fulfilment of time, that God's kingdom would only come at the end of the material world, made me see the possibility that *Revelation* would be the visionary panoramic picture of its realisation. During the process of translating it, I became convinced of the traditional view that St. John wrote it. I know that this is not the modern scholarly judgement because of the difference in style. In defence of my own intuition, I cannot help but think of C.S. Lewis who wrote erudite and logical arguments on behalf of the Christian faith; yet was still able to create the vision of the land of Narnia, where the lion Aslan inspires children in their battle for the triumph of goodness in themselves and in the magical world to which they have been transposed by walking through a wardrobe. Had the initials 'C.S.' been erased from all the copies of his works, who would have believed that the same Lewis had been the author of such philosophy and fantasy? I believe it is the same John, whether he is called St. John or John the Divine of Patmos.

Whether they like it or not, readers will have to appreciate that the major thrust of the NT is that those who make physical comfort their chief goal, and view spiritual interests and good deeds as secondary aims once they have achieved the first, have no place by the side of the Christian God. Jesus demands a young man who keeps all the ethical commandments to give all his wealth to the poor. St. Matthew says that he went away sadly because he was very rich. Jesus is recorded as commenting that it easier for a camel to go through the eye of a needle than for a rich man to enter the Kingdom of Heaven. In other words, the rich young man's righteousness counted for little. For Sigmund Freud, the life force expressed itself in the desire for wealth, status and the love of women. The rabbis of antiquity told a story; there was delight in the community when the evil urge was arrested and locked up until it was discovered that from that moment chickens stopped laying eggs. The sages commented that, without the evil urge, people would not marry, build houses and go into business. Jesus's message, at least as portrayed in parts of the synoptic gospels, all of *St. John* and *Revelation*, is that living a worldly life is not the admission ticket to God's Kingdom.

Once one comes to grip with the author's theological stance, namely that the triumph over the human evils of ambition, greed and lust cannot be achieved in the world ruled by Satan; that the battle for the triumph of goodness is one to be fought by cosmic combatants and that the human faithful achieve their personal salvation by commitment to the right side, it can become no less an exciting read than the fantasies of Tolkien. In fact, one can say even better, first because its symbolism has greater profundity, and secondly it is much shorter. The images are incredibly horrific and wonderful, and based to some extent on mystical revelations found in Old Testament books.

Traditional Christianity, as I have already intimated, is very ambivalent about *Revelation*. Its description of the Apocalypse leads *The Oxford Dictionary of the Christian Religion* to make this concluding comment about the book:

> But its importance and potentially dangerous impact stem from its futuristic eschatology and the use made of it by millenarians of all periods, including Jehovah's Witnesses and esp. fundamentalist Protestants today.

While translating the book, I felt that it was doing no more than developing the Apocalyptic nature of classic Christianity to its ultimate fulfilment, but that its theology – root and branch – is about God's victory through Christ but only at the End of Days. Perhaps, it was for this very reason that the Church hierarchy in tandem with the secular authorities feared that the disclosure of the Bible to ordinary men and women would reveal the hypocrisy of the princes of the Church and State because of their exultation in personal wealth, status and worldly power.

Appreciation of this work should not depend on whether you are a Christian or not. So long as you enjoy fables of the future, you will want to enter the imaginative and magical world of John the Divine which he fills with wild, weird and wonderful creatures and angels who are engaged in the final battles between good and evil. Whatever one's beliefs, the writing evokes visual pictures which has inspired artists for centuries and is still fertile ground for painters of the occult. Equally, faith is irrelevant to the pleasure the reader can obtain by probing the mysteries of the wealth of symbols and images.

But, however you read it, the reader should be clear about its deeper moral message: that those who wish to embrace the life of the spirit and to assure God his final victory will have to sacrifice their natural human appetites and join Jesus in the city of angels, where, once the battle is won, they too might sit on heavenly thrones next to Jesus and his apostles, forever singing praises to God – the creator of all.

1 The revelation of the future

A revelation of Jesus Christ which God gave to Him
To show his servants what is soon to happen.
This he did by sending it through his Angel
To John, his servant[1], who bore witness to everything he saw:
The word of God and the witnessing of Jesus Christ.
Blessed is he who reads and hears these words of prophesy
And who is mindful of what is written in it because the time is
     near!

From John to the seven Churches[2] in Asia:
Grace to you and peace from
He who is, who was and who is to come[3]
And from the seven spirits who are by his throne
And from Jesus Christ, the faithful witness,
The first-born of the dead[4]
And ruler of the kings of the earth.

To Him who loved us and freed us from our sins by his blood,
And made us into a kingdom of priests to God his father.
His is the glory and the power forever and ever. Amen.
Look, he comes upon the clouds;[5]

[1] The implication is that this is John the Apostle.
[2] The Greek *ekklaysia* is always translated as church. Its literal meaning is
'assembly', 'congregation' or 'community'. It came to mean a 'circle' or body of
Christians. As St. Paul perceived each 'holy community' as the body of Christ,
the Church became a mystical entity.
[3] From what follows, this would not be Jesus but God the Father. His
description resonates with God telling Moses that his name is
Ehyeh-asher-ehyeh, 'I will be what I will be'.
[4] The Pharisees believed in the resurrection of the dead. When St. Paul defends
his faith in Christ, he maintains that the Resurrection is in keeping with Jewish
belief. Jesus, therefore, is the first to enjoy bodily resurrection, and therefore,
the first-born of the dead.
[5] In *Daniel 7:13*, he sees 'as it were a son of man' coming on the clouds. Jesus
was identified with him.

Every eye will see Him, even those who pierced Him.
All the peoples of the earth will mourn over Him.

"I am the Alpha and the Omega," says the Lord God,
The one who is, the one who was and the one who is to
 come –
The Almighty.

I, John, your brother and partner in the affliction, the kingdom
 and endurance of Jesus, happened to be in Patmos because
 of the word of God, to give witness to Jesus.

Jesus appears to John

On the Lord's Day I was inspired and heard behind me a voice
As loud as a trumpet saying, "Write what you see on a scroll
And send it to the seven Churches: Ephesus, Smyrna,
Pergamum, Thyatira, Sardis, Philadelphia and Laodicia."
I turned around to see the voice speaking to me.
When I turned, I saw seven golden lamp stands.[1]
Among the lamp stands was as it were a Son of Man,[2]
Clothed down to his feet with a golden sash around his chest.
His head and hair were white as wool, white as snow
And his eyes blazed like fire;
His feet gleamed like brass glowing in a furnace.
His voice was like the waves of rushing waters.
He held seven stars in his right hand;
Out of his mouth came a sharp double-edged sword.
His face was shining with a power equal to the sun.

When I saw Him, I collapsed at his feet as though dead.
He put his right hand on me and said, "Be not afraid.

---

[1] The candlestick of the Tabernacle built in the wilderness by Moses had a central stem and three on either side (*Exodus* 25:37) Here, the seven lamp stands represent the seven Churches. It may be significant that St. Paul in his letters addresses seven Communities. As there are seven days in the week, the number seven expressed a unity whose apex was the Sabbath.
[2] See fn. 5 on previous page.

I am the first and the last – the living one; I died but see,
I live now for all ages holding the keys of death and Hades.
Write, therefore, what you have seen, what you see now
And those things that are soon to occur.
The mystery of the seven stars you saw in my right hand
And the seven lamp stands has this explanation:
The seven stars are the Angels[1] of the seven Churches
And the lamp stands are the seven Churches."

2 John writes to the Churches in the name of Jesus

Write to the head of the Church in Ephesus:
He who holds the seven stars in his right hand;
He who walks amidst the seven golden lamps stands,
Says these words: I know of your hard work and
    perseverance;
That you cannot tolerate evil men and have challenged
Those who called themselves apostles[2] but are not;
Whom you discovered to be liars.
You have persevered and suffered for the sake of my name.
And have not grown weary. But, I hold this against you:
You have forsaken your first love[3];
Remember the height from which you have fallen;
Repent and return to your early efforts. If you do not,
I will come to you and remove your lamp stand from its place,

[1] The reader should be reminded that 'Angel' is a derivative of the Greek *Angellos* meaning 'messenger'. In the next chapter, from its context, it would appear that they are the rulers of the seven Churches.
[2] Who are they? With the exception of St. Paul, to whom Jesus appeared, the apostles were the twelve who witnessed Jesus. St. Paul also writes of false apostles in *11 Corinthians* ch. 11.
[3] From the preceding line, the 'first love' could not be Jesus. Was it St. Paul who made a great impact in Ephesus (*Acts*, ch.19)? His letter to the Ephesians is very significant as it emphasises the doctrine that St. John develops: Christians are redeemed through the blood of Jesus and through Him become God's adopted children. In this letter, he also stresses his mission as the apostle to the Gentiles and the negation of the laws of the Torah as the way to God.

Unless you repent! But, to your credit, you hate,
The practices of the Nicolaitans[1], as I do.

Let Him who has an ear hear what the **Divine** Spirit
Says to the Churches: To Him, who is victorious,[2]
I will grant the right to eat of the Tree of Life,
Which is in the paradise[3] of God.

Write to the head of the Church in Smyrna.
These are the words of he who is the first and the last,
Who died and lived again: I know your affliction and poverty,
But you are rich. I know of the slander of those who are not
But call themselves Jews–they are a meeting place[4] for Satan.
Do not be afraid of what you are about to suffer.
The devil will put some of you into prison to test you.
You will suffer for ten days. Be faithful until death and
I will grant you the crown of **eternal** life.
Let Him who has an ear hear what the **Divine** Spirit says
To the Churches: he who is victorious
Will not suffer any hurt by the second death.[5]

Write to the head of the Church in Pergamum.
These are the words of Him who has a sharp double-edged sword:

---

[1] These are the followers of Nicolas, who might have been one of the seven disciples who was chosen to look after the administration of the Church while the apostles got on with spreading the word. Nicolas is identified as a Jewish proselyte from Antioch. While most scholars consider this identification as merely speculative, I think it makes sense. Nicolas, who went to efforts to convert to Judaism before following Jesus, would have, like St. Peter, valued the Jewish rites and traditions. He could well have rejected the de-Judaization of Christianity by viewing the Messiah-king as God incarnate.

[2] Literally: 'overcomes'– those who, like Jesus, remain steadfast in their faith in Christ in spite of persecution.

[3] Paradise in Greek means garden or playground.

[4] The Greek is *sunagogay* which is synagogue, meaning meeting place. Synagogue, in fact, is the Greek translation of the Hebrew *Bet Knesset*, which has the same meaning. In view of the fact that they were not, according to Jesus, Jews, I have decided not to translate it in a pejorative manner.

[5] This expression only occurs in *Revelation*. It may refer to the sufferings in hell, which would be the equivalent of a second and worse death, but see p. 145 fn no. 1.

I know where you live, where Satan has his throne.
Still, you hold fast to my name, nor did you deny faith in
   me even at the time of Antipas, my faithful witness
Who was killed among you – where Satan lives.
But, I do have a few things against you.
Among you are a few, who follow the teaching of Balaam,
Who taught Balak to put a stumbling block before Israel –
To eat sacrifices to idols and to commit fornication.[1]
And you have some following the teaching of the Nicolaitans.
Therefore, repent; otherwise I will soon come to you and
Will fight against them with the sword of my mouth.

Let him who has an ear hear what the **Divine** Spirit
Says to the Churches: to him, who is victorious,
I will give some of the hidden manna;[2] I will also give him
A white stone[3] on which will be written a new name,[4]
Which no one will know except he who receives it.[5]

Write to the head of the Church in Thyatira.
These are the words of the Son of God
Whose eyes blazed like fire;
And whose feet were like gleaming brass:
I know your works, your love, your faith, your ministry and
Your perseverance; that you now do more than you first did.

[1] The prophet Balaam was employed by Balak, the king of Moab, to curse the Israelites. Instead, he blesses them but his held responsible for their idolatrous behaviour at Baal Peor, see *Numbers* ch. 25

[2] In *Psalms* 78:24–25, mannah is described as coming down from heaven and being the food of the mighty, e.g. God's celestial companions. St. John also describes Jesus as the bread of life. The imagery suggests the gift of the food of the immortals.

[3] Stones were used by judges or officials to mark acquittal or condemnation; also as tickets into privileged societies. This may have been an indication of Jesus's approval for entry into God's kingdom.

[4] A new name is the sign of divine blessing. Abram becomes Abraham to signify that he will become a father of many nations. Jacob is named Israel after he has defeated a divine figure.

[5] Knowledge of a person's name can give magical power to others over the named person. The secret name is a sign of love between Christ and the faithful one.

But I have this against you: you tolerate the woman, Jezebel,
Who claims to be a prophetess; she teaches and misleads
My servants to commit fornication and eat sacrifices to idols.
I gave her time to repent; she will not repent of her fornication.
See, I am casting her into a bed **of suffering;**
And I will afflict those who have committed adultery with
    her.
Unless they repent of her ways, I will kill her children.[1]
Then, all the Churches will know that I am he
Who searches the hearts and minds[2]
And will repay each of you according to your deeds.[3]

But to the rest of you in Thyatira, who do not follow
This teaching **of Jezebel,** who have not plumbed, as they say,
The secret depths of Satan[4], I will not subject you
To any further strictures; just hold fast
To what you have until I come.[5]
To Him who is victorious and keeps working for me
Until the end, I will grant authority over the nations.
He will shepherd them with a rod of iron;

---

[1] It is extraordinary that such an utterance could be included in the last
volume of the New Testament. Ezekiel rejects the concept of children suffering
for the sins of their parents, yet the biblical threat of punishment against one's
offspring, as a deterrent to bad behaviour, remains prevalent in the Christian
era. As I point out in my previous translations of the Old Testament, so long as
children were primarily seen as the continuation of the ancestral line, and not
as individuals in their own right, collective family responsibility could not be
avoided, even in the most advanced religious faiths.

[2] Literally: kidneys and hearts; the former was seen to be the seat of the
emotions, and the latter the seat of intelligence.

[3] It is hard to distinguish the punishing Christ portrayed here from that of
God of the Old Testament, much maligned by Christians throughout the
centuries.

[4] This is fascinating. St. Paul in his letters also attacks the sexual
permissiveness in the Churches. New sects which focussed on the cult of the
individual, living in closed communities without a code of law, often preached
the achievement of salvation through sexual orgies, perhaps because the sexual
act can give such a liberating sense of power and unity.

[5] If John is writing this on behalf of Christ, the implication is that it is Jesus
who is promising to visit Thyatira.

Like clay pots they will be shattered[1] –
Just as I have received **authority** from my father.
I will grant Him the morning star.
Let Him who has an ear hear what
The **Divine** Spirit says to the Churches.[2]

3 Jesus rebukes only those he loves

Write to the head of the Church in Sardis:
These are the words of he who owns
The seven spirits of God and the seven stars:
I know your deeds; you enjoy the appearance of being alive,
But in reality you are dead. Be wary!
Strengthen what remains, that which is soon to die.[3]
To my finding, your deeds are not perfect
In the sight of my God; remember, therefore,
What you have received and heard. Obey and repent!
If you are not on guard, I will come like a thief and
You will not know the time of my coming to you.[4]

Yet, some among you in Sardis have not defiled their clothes;
They shall walk with me in white because they are worthy.
He who is victorious will, like them, be dressed in white;
Nor will I blot out his name from the Book of Life.
I will recommend his name before my father and his Angels.[5]

---

[1] These two lines are a paraphrase of *Psalms 2:9*: 'You shall break them with a rod of iron; you shall dash them into pieces like a potters vessel.' The second psalm is very significant in Christology as it describes the uprising against the Lord and his Messiah-king. In our text, there is an irony in a shepherd, who is meant to be gentle with his sheep, using an iron rod to punish them.

[2] This is the clearest indication that the believers are being promised through their faith to share equally in the powers that God the Father has given to Christ.

[3] The message is: the years are passing; repent before your death.

[4] These are also the words ascribed to Jesus in *St Matthew 24:42–44* and in *St. Luke 12:39–40*: the faithful must be ready for the coming of the Son of Man, for he will come like an unexpected thief.

[5] This suborns Christ's position for he as the Son of God and god incarnate is superior to the Angels.

Let Him with an ear hear what
The Divine Spirit says to the Churches.

Write to the head of the Church of Philadelphia:
These are the words of the holy one, the true one,
He who has the key of David.
What he opens, none can shut; what he shuts, none can
    open.
I know your deeds. I have put before you an open door that
No one can shut; you have little strength,
Yet you kept my teaching and did not deny my name.
I will make those of the assembly of Satan who say
They are Jews when they are not, but are liars.
I will make them come and worship at your feet
And they shall know that I loved you; because
You obeyed my teaching to persevere on my account,
I will also protect you from the hour of trial that is coming
To the entire world to test those who live on the earth.

I am coming very soon; hold fast to what you have,
So that no one will steal your crown.
I will make a pillar of him who is victorious in the Temple of
    my God; he will never leave.
I will inscribe on him the name of my God and the name of
    the city of my God –
The New Jerusalem sent down from heaven by my God.
And **I will inscribe on him** my new name.
Let him who has an ear hear
What the **Divine** Spirit says to the Churches.

Write to the head of the Church in Laodicia:
These are the words of Amen[1], the faithful and true witness,
The sovereign of God's creation.

---

[1] This must be Jesus as he is God's witness. Amen means faithfulness or true in
the sense of loyal. Isaiah speaks of the God of amen (65:16) i.e. the God of
truth. 'Amen' as the conclusion of a declaration or a prayer is an affirmative:
verily so.

I know your deeds – they are neither hot nor cold!
Because you are lukewarm – neither hot nor cold –
I am about to vomit you out of my mouth,
Because you say, "I am rich, I have become rich
And I have no **material** needs" and do not know that
You are wretched, to be pitied, poor, blind and naked.
I advise you to buy from me gold refined in fire
To become rich and to be dressed in white,
So that the shame of your nakedness may be covered –
And to apply balm to your eyes so that you may see.

It is only those I love that I rebuke and reprove:
Therefore, be hot and repent!
See, I stand at the door and knock.
If anyone hears my voice and opens the door,
I will go and eat with him and him with me.
I will allow him who is victorious to sit on my throne
Just as I was victorious and sat with my father on his Throne.[1]
Let him who has an ear hear what
The **Divine** Spirit says to the Churches.

4 God and his Throne

After this I looked – a door stood open in heaven.
And the voice I heard speaking to me as loud as thunder,
"Come up here and I will show you what will happen after
    this."
In an instant, I joined the spiritual world.
There was a Throne in heaven and on it sat one[2] who looked
    like jasper and carnelian.
A rainbow around the Throne shone like a sapphire.

---

[1] This is a further confirmation of the promise of St. Paul's promise that all those who believe and participate in Christ become like Him.
[2] Why is John not prepared to call Him God? Perhaps, because he is aware that this is a vision, not to be taken literally. If God could sit on a throne like a human king, how would he be different than Zeus and all the pagan gods deplored by Judaism and the Christian apostles!

Encircling the Throne were twenty-four other thrones.
Twenty-four Elders[1] dressed in white sat on them.
Golden crowns adorned their heads.
The Throne shot out a flash of lightning and a clapping of thunder.
Seven lamps were burning at the foot of the throne;
These were the seven spirits[2] of God.

The Four Living Creatures

The floor under the Throne was like a sea of glass – clear as
    crystal.
Four Living Creatures[3] covered with eyes – front and back –
    stood around the Throne.
The first Living Creature looked like a lion;
The second Living Creature like an ox;
The third Living Creature had the face of a man;
The fourth Living Creature like an eagle ready to soar.[4]
Each of the four had six wings fully covered with eyes.[5]

Without resting, they kept declaring day and night,
"Holy, holy, holy is the Lord God, the almighty one,
Who was, who is and who is to come."
Whenever the Living Creatures render glory, honour and
    thanks to Him

---

[1] In *St. Matthew* 19:28 and *St. Luke* 22:30, Jesus promises the apostles that
they will sit on twelve thrones beside him to judge the tribes of Israel. The
other twelve could be the heads of the tribes of Israel; this would reflect the
identification of the old with the new Israel.
[2] These are the seven aspects or manifestations of God, often reflected in the
functions of the seven archangels, of which more later.
[3] These four creatures, which look like a lion, an ox, a human and an eagle,
are based on Ezekiel's vision at the beginning of his prophecy. Daniel also had
a vision of four beasts; a lion, a bear, a leopard, the fourth without any
likeness but with ten horns and a little horn among them, *Daniel* 7:2–8.
[4] The creatures appear to reflect the different categories of God's domain:
untamed animals, tamed animals, humans and heavenly spirits. I think the
eagle reflects the latter, rather than birds, as, if this was the intention, one
would expect a creature in the form of a fish.
[5] The eyes are also based on Ezekiel's vision of the four creatures, except, in the
case of Ezekiel's, they are not fully covered with eyes.

Who is seated on the Throne and lives forever and ever, the
Twenty-four Elders fall on their faces before Him,
Who is seated on the Throne, and worship Him who lives
    forever and ever.
They lay down their crowns before Him and declare,
"You are worthy, our Lord and God, to receive the glory and
    honour and power
Because you create all things and it is only by your will that
    they were created."

5 The scroll and the glorification of the Lamb

In the right hand of Him who sat on the Throne, I saw a
Scroll with writing on both sides, sealed with seven seals.
I saw a mighty Angel proclaiming in a loud voice,
"Who is worthy to open the scroll by breaking its seals?"
No one in heaven, or on earth, or underneath the earth was
    able to open the scroll to look inside it.
I could not stop weeping because no one was worthy enough
To open the scroll to look inside it.
An Elder said to me, "Weep not, and see the Lion of the tribe
    of Judah, the shoot of David has triumphed –
To open the scroll by breaking its seven seals."

By the Throne and the four Living Creatures and the Elders,
I saw a Lamb looking as if it had been killed[1] with
Seven horns and seven eyes which are the Spirits of God,
Which he sent forth throughout the world.
He came and took it from the right hand of Him who sat on
    the throne; as he took the scroll,
The four Living Creatures and the twenty-four Elders
Fell on their faces before the Lamb, each with a harp

[1] Jesus, as both the Lion – the conquering Messiah king from the House of
David – and the Lamb, God's beloved Son who was chosen to be sacrificed for
the redemption of a sinful humanity, is a paradox, with which the founders of

And a golden bowl of incense with which the Holy Ones do worship.

They sang a new song with these words,
"You are worthy to receive the scroll and break its seals
Because you were killed and by your blood,
You acquired men from every tribe and tongue,
And from every people and nation for God,
By making them serve God as a Kingdom of Priests –
So that they would reign on earth."[1]
I looked and heard the cry of many Angels around the Throne,
As well as the Living Creatures and the Elders numbering
Thousands upon thousands, myriads upon myriads shouting,
"Worthy is the Lamb who was slain to receive
The power and the riches, the wisdom and strength,
The honour, glory and praise."[2]
I heard every creature in heaven and on earth and
Underneath the earth and in the sea – everything in them –
Saying, "To Him seated on the Throne and to the Lamb,
Be praise and honour, glory and power forever and ever."
The four Living Creatures said, "Amen."
The Elders prostrated themselves and worshipped.

6 The opening of the first seal – the White Horse

I saw the Lamb break open the first of the seven seals;
I heard one of the four Living Creatures speaking as thunder,
"Come!" I then saw a white horse; its rider had a bow.
He was given a crown and rode forth to win victories.[3]

Christianity wrestled and finally resolved by viewing his death as a victory.
Jesus as God's son is also the body of his seven spirits.

[1] This is what God promises the Israelites in the wilderness: that they will be 'a kingdom of priests, a dedicated (holy) people, see *Exodus 19:6*.

[2] The reader should note that the divine gifts number seven.

[3] Each seal contains a chapter, but the words become a picture – the modern video. The white horse is the symbol of war. The horses that follow will be the devastating consequences of war.

The opening of the second seal – the Scarlet Horse

When the Lamb broke open the second seal,
I heard the second Living Creature say, "Come!"
And out came another horse – a scarlet one.
Its rider was dispatched to remove peace from the earth,
To make men kill one another.
He was given a great sword.

The opening of the third seal – the Black Horse

When he opened the third seal,
I heard the third Living Creature say, "Come!"
I saw a black horse; its rider had scales in his hands.
I heard a voice from among the four Living Creatures, saying,
"A measure of wheat for a denarius,
Three measures of barley for a denarius.
Do not even touch the wine or oil."[1]

The opening of the fourth seal – the Pale Green Horse

When he opened the fourth seal,
I heard the voice of the fourth Living Creature say, "Come!
I saw a pale green horse; its rider's name was death[2]
And Hades[3] was following **at his heels.**
They were given control over a quarter of the earth
To kill by the sword, by famine, by death **from disease**
And by the wild beasts of the earth.[4]

---

[1] War and destruction lead to scarcity and inflation. According to *Matthew 20:2*, a labourer's daily wage was a denarius. While the labourer might be able barely to afford bread, wine and oil would be totally beyond his reach.
[2] The horse's colour is a sickly green because disease will be the consequence of corpses and famine.
[3] The Greek underworld; Hades is pictured as the 'great reaper'.
[4] The devastation would be so great that towns would attract animal scavengers.

The opening of the fifth seal – the plea of the Martyrs

When he broke open the fifth seal,
I saw underneath the altar[1] the souls of those killed
Because they obeyed the word of God and bore witness to it.
They were crying out with loud voices,
"Until when, O divine and true sovereign, will you wait
Before judging the dwellers on earth and avenge our blood?"
Each of them was given a white robe and told to wait awhile,
Until the killing of their fellow servants would be completed.[2]

The opening of the sixth seal – Judgement Day

I watched as he broke open the sixth seal,
There occurred a great earthquake.
The sun became as black as sackcloth made of hair;
And the entire moon turned into blood.
Like unripe figs cast off by a fig tree when shaken by a
strong wind, heaven's stars fell to the ground.
The heavens receded like a scroll being rolled up.
Every mountain and island was moved from its place.
Then the kings of the earth, the nobleman and generals,
The rich and the mighty, every slave and freeman hid
themselves in the caves and crags of mountains.
They cried out to the mountains and crags,
"Fall down on us and hide us from the face of Him seated on
the Throne,
And from the wrath of the Lamb because the great day of their
wrath has come.
Who can withstand it?"

---

[1] This is an appropriate image because like Jesus they died as sacrifices on his behalf.
[2] This was the self-comfort of those martyrs under Rome seeking to comprehend why the almighty God was not punishing their persecutors.

7 Interlude: the four Angels – the reward of the faithful

After this I saw four Angels standing on the four corners of the earth,[1]
Restraining the four winds of the earth from blowing
On any land, on the seas or on any tree.
I saw another Angel arising from the East
Holding the **protective** seal[2] of the Living God.
The Angel called out in a loud voice to the four Angels
Who were designated to attack the land and the sea,
"Do not harm the land or the sea or the trees until
We put a seal on the foreheads of the servants of our God.
Then I heard the number of those who had been sealed –
One hundred and forty four thousand from all the tribes of Israel:[3]
 From the tribe of Judah – 12,000 had been sealed;
 From the tribe of Reuben – 12,000 had been sealed;
 From the tribe of Gad – 12,000 had been sealed;
 From the tribe of Asher – 12,000 had been sealed;
 From the tribe of Naphtali – 12,000 had been sealed;
 From the tribe of Manasseh – 12,000 had been sealed;
 From the tribe of Simeon – 12,000 had been sealed;

---

[1] The number four is the most ubiquitous number: not only the four corners of the earth, but North, South, East and West – the four winds connected to these directions, four seasons, four parts of the day. The symbolic quality of the number leads to the popularity of forty to suggest a long time: forty days and nights of the great flood, Moses spending forty days on Mount Sinai, and the Israelites wandering in the wilderness for forty years.

[2] In *Ezekiel* 9, the non-idolators' foreheads are marked to save them from divine destruction.

[3] Explanations have been sought for the absence of the tribe of Dan, the listing of the tribe of Joseph, the ancestor of the two tribes of Ephraim and Manasseh, instead of listing Ephraim, as Manasseh is included. Also the tribes are not listed in their genealogical order. I choose to believe that the narrator, not that keen on historical accuracy, but on the metaphor, was writing from the top of his head. One would have expected an editor to have corrected the list, but the dire warning against changing anything at the conclusion of *Revelation* may have been taken too seriously.

From the tribe of Levi – 12,000 had been sealed;
From the tribe of Issachar – 12,000 had been sealed;
From the tribe of Zebulun – 12,000 had been sealed;
From the tribe of Joseph – 12,000 had been sealed;
From the tribe of Benjamin – 12,000 had been sealed.

After this, I saw a crowd beyond numbering from every nation,
    tribe, people and tongue,
Standing before the Throne and before the Lamb,
Clothed in white robes holding palms in their hands.
They shouted with a loud voice,
"Salvation belongs to our God –
To Him seated on the Throne and to the Lamb."
All the Angels who stood around the Throne and the Elders
    and the four Living Creatures fell on their faces
    before the Throne and worshipped God, declaring,
"Amen, praise, glory, wisdom and thanksgiving, honour,
Power and strength to our God forever and ever. Amen."
Then one of the Elders asked me,
"These dressed in white robes, who are they and from where
    do they come?"
I answered, "My lord, you know." He told me,
"These are those from the great tribulation; they have
Washed and whitened their clothes in the blood of the Lamb.[1]
Therefore, they are before the Throne of God
And serve him day and night in his Temple.
He who sits on the Throne will spread his Tent over them.
They will no longer hunger or thirst;
They will not be harmed by the sun or heat,
Because the Lamb at the centre of the Throne will shepherd
    them and guide them to springs of living waters,
And God will wipe away every tear from their eyes."[2]

---

[1] Washing one's clothes in blood is an image revealing the paradox of the
victory over sin caused by the blood of the sacrifice of Jesus.
[2] *Isaiah 25:8* is the origin of this line.

8 The opening of the seventh seal – the Seven Angels

When the Lamb broke open the seventh seal,
There was silence in heaven for about half an hour.
I saw the Seven Angels who stand before God;[1]
They were given seven trumpets.
Another Angel, holding a gold censer stood before the altar.
He was given much incense **to offer** with the prayers of
All the Holy Ones on the golden Altar before the Throne.
The smoke of the incense, along with the prayers of the
Holy Ones rose up to God from the hand of the Angel.
Then the Angel took the censer, filled it with fire from the altar
  and threw it to the ground.
And there were peals of thunder and rumblings
And flashes of lightning and an earthquake.[2]

The sounding of the first Angel

The seven Angels with the trumpets prepared to sound them.
The first Angel sounded his trumpet:
Hail and fire mixed with blood were hurled to the ground.
A third of the earth was burnt up –
A third of the trees were burnt up,
And all the vegetation was burnt up.

The sounding of the second Angel

The second Angel sounded his trumpet:
Something like a great burning mountain was cast into the
  sea.

---

[1] The apocryphal book *Tobit* (12:15) refers to Raphael as one of the seven archangels who are the intermediaries between the righteous and God. According to Jewish tradition, they each had a special function. Their names are: Uriel, Raphael, Raguel, Michael, Sariel, Gabriel and Jeremiel.
[2] It would appear that the prayers were for divine punishment for those who had persecuted them and for those who had rejected Christ. The petition is granted.

A third of the sea turned into blood and a third of living
creatures died in the sea.
And a third of all the ships were destroyed.

The sounding of the third Angel

The third Angel sounded his trumpet:
A large star burning like a lamp fell into a third of the rivers
and water springs.
The name of the star was Wormwood (bitterness),
So a third of the waters became bitter,
And many peoples died from the bitter waters.

The sounding of the fourth Angel

The fourth Angel sounded his trumpet:
A third of the sun and a third of the moon and a third of the
stars were stricken so that a third of them turned dark.
And so a third of the day would be dark, and so with the
night.

The warning from the Eagle

And I saw and heard an eagle flying in the middle of heaven
Crying out in a loud voice: "Woe, woe, woe[1] to the inhabitants
of the earth,
Because of the other trumpet blasts, still to be sounded by the
other three Angels."[2]

9 The sounding of the fifth Angel

The fifth angel sounded his trumpet:
I saw a star that had fallen from the heavens to the earth.

---

[1] The three woes are to be linked to the soundings of the latter three angels.
[2] The trumpet blasts of the first four angels led to the spoiling of nature. The
next two blasts will be directed against humanity and the final one will be to
announce the Kingdom of God, but there are many interventions in the
narrative before then.

It had been given the key to the shaft of the abyss;
Smoke rose from it like that from a great furnace.
The sun and air were darkened by the smoke from the shaft.
Locusts[1] emerged from the smoke and swarmed over the
  earth.
They were granted the control possessed by the scorpions of
  the earth.
They were ordered not to damage the vegetation of the land –
No plants or trees – only men without the seal of God on their
  foreheads.

The army of locusts – the first Woe

They were not permitted to kill them – only to torment them
  for five months.
Their pain was like that suffered by a person stung by a
  scorpion.
During those days, men will seek death but will not find
  it;
They will long to die but death will elude them.
The locusts will look like horses ready for battle.
On their heads were what looked like golden crowns.
Their faces were those resembling men;
Their hair like that of women;
Their teeth like those of lions;
Their breastplates were of iron;
The sounds of their wings like the clamouring of many horses
  rushing into battle;
Their tails and stings like those of scorpions.
As their commander, they had the Angel of the Abyss,
In Hebrew called, Abbadon – **Destroyer** – in Greek, Appolyon.

---

[1] The reader may have noticed that some of the afflictions are similar to
those of the ten plagues suffered by the Egyptians: blood, darkness and now
locusts.

The sounding of the sixth Angel – the second Woe – Four Angels released for battle

One cause for woe having passed, two were still to come.
The sixth Angel sounded his trumpet:
I heard a voice calling out to the sixth Angel, holding the
   trumpet from the centre of the four horns of the golden
   altar before God:
"Let loose the four Angels at the great river, Euphrates."
The four Angels who were ready for the hour and the day,
The month and the year were set free to kill a third of Man.
The number of mounted men was two myriads of myriads[1].

The Divine Cavalry and the desolation it inflicts

This is how the horses and their riders looked in my vision:
Their breastplates were fiery red, dark blue and yellow like
   sulphur.
The heads of the horses were like those of lions;
Their mouths were fuming fire, smoke and sulphur.
A third of mankind was killed by the three afflictions
Caused by the fire, smoke and sulphur, which spewed from
   their mouths.
The destructive power of the horses was in their mouths and
   tails,
For their tails were like those of serpents with heads on them,
   with which they inflicted injuries.
The rest of mankind who were not killed by these afflictions
Were still not moved to repent of the works of their hands.
They persisted in worshipping demons and idols of gold and
   silver, bronze and stone and wood.
Which neither see, nor hear nor walk.
They did not repent of their murderous acts, their sorceries,
   their fornications and robberies.

[1] 200 million.

10 The intervention of a mighty Angel with the bittersweet scroll

I saw yet another mighty angel coming down from heaven,
Clothed in a cloud with a rainbow above his head.
His face was like the sun; his feet like pillars of fire.
In his hand was a small unrolled scroll.
He planted his right foot on the sea and his left foot on land.
He cried out with a voice as loud as the roar of a lion.
When he cried out, the Seven Thunders[1] spoke with their own
    voices.
When the Seven Thunders spoke, I was about to write it
    down,
But I heard a voice from heaven say,
"Put a seal on what the Seven Thunders said;
You may not write it down."

The Angel whom I saw standing on the sea and on the land,
Raised his right hand to heaven and swore by him
Who lives forever and ever, who created the heavens
And all that is in them and the earth and all that is in it,
And the sea and all that is in it, and declared,
"There is to be no further delay; at the time of the voice of the
    seventh Angel, whenever he sounds his trumpet,
The mystery of God will be accomplished just as he declared to
    his servants and prophets."

The voice I heard speaking out of heaven spoke to me again:
"Go, take the scroll that lies open in the hand of the Angel
    who stands on the sea and the land."
I approached the Angel and asked him for the small scroll.
He said, "Take it and eat it; it will turn your stomach sour,
But in your mouth, it will be as sweet as honey."
I took the small scroll from the Angel's hand and ate it;

---

[1] I think we must suppose that these reflect divine judgement. The number seven, as is indicated throughout, reflects completeness and fulfilment.

It tasted in my mouth as sweet as honey but when I ate it, it
turned my stomach sour.
And they, **the voices of the Seven Thunders,** said to me,
"You must again prophesy about many peoples and nations,
tongues and kings."

11 The Prophecy, destruction and resurrection of the two witnesses

I was given a reed to use as a measuring rod and told,
"Go, measure the Temple of God, the altar and those
worshipping in it.[1]
Do not measure the court outside the Temple because it has
been handed over to the Gentiles.
They[2] will trample on the holy city for forty-two months.
I will appoint two of my witnesses,[3] who will prophesy,
Clothed in sackcloth for one thousand, two hundred and sixty
days.[4]
These are **symbolised by** the two olive trees and the two lamp
stands that stood before the Lord of the earth.
If anyone tries to harm them, fire spews from their mouths to
devour their enemies.
Anyone who tries to harm them – this is the way they die.

---

[1] *Ezekiel,* see chs. 40–42 is also ordered in a vision to measure the Temple. To
number the worshippers a line or rod was drawn alongside them and an
estimate was achieved. It was considered bad luck to number people. It can be
assumed that the purpose was to protect those within the Temple.
[2] These must be the Gentiles.
[3] According to biblical law, two witnesses are required to verify a matter, see
People's Bible: Moses, Book 2: The Laws of Moses, p.147 or *Deuteronomy* 17:6.
The two required witnesses are often used figuratively: the two tablets of the
law are witnesses of the covenant made between God and Israel, see ibid Book
1: *Moses, Man of God,* p. 55 (*Exodus* 31:18). Also God calls heaven and earth
as witnesses to his covenant with Israel, ibid p. 158 (*Deut.* 30:19)
[4] On the assumption that a month was made up of thirty days, this would be
the equivalent of the forty-two months of persecution by the Gentiles. The sum
is also the equivalent of 180 weeks, the relevance of which appears later in the
text.

Theirs is the power to seal the sky so that it ceases to rain
    while they prophesy.
Theirs is the power over the waters to turn them into blood
And to strike the earth with every kind of affliction whenever
    they wish.

When they complete their testimony,
The Beast who arises from the Abyss will kill them.[1]
Their corpses will lie on the main street of the great city,
Figuratively,[2] known as Sodom or Egypt –
Indeed where their Lord was crucified.[3]
The peoples and tribes, tongues and nations
Do not permit their burial,
So that they can look at them for three and a half days.
The inhabitants of earth gloat over them;
They rejoice and exchange presents with each other,
Because these two prophets had tormented them.

After three and a half days, God's breath of life entered them.
They rose to their feet and a great fright struck those who had
    been staring at them.
They heard a loud voice booming at them from heaven,
"Come up here!" They rose up to heaven in a cloud in the
    sight of their enemies.
At that moment, there was a great earthquake;
A tenth of the city collapsed and seven thousand people were
    killed by the earthquake.
The others were terrified and gave glory to the God of heaven.
So the second woe passed; the third woe is soon to come.

---

[1] The Beast will be identified later; it is significant, that in spite of their powers just described, they are killed – further indication that their deaths are part of the divine plan as a prelude to their resurrection.

[2] This is also a significant indication that John's visions are not intended to be taken literally.

[3] As 'their Lord' could only be Jesus and we know that he was crucified in a neighbourhood of Jerusalem, the substitution of Sodom, the city of sin, and Egypt, the land of Israel's bondage, suggests that God's witnesses are constantly being slaughtered throughout the wicked world.

The sounding of the seventh Angel:
Judgement Day and The Kingdom of God

The seventh Angel sounded his trumpet;
Loud voices were heard in heaven,
"The kingdom of the world has been transformed into
The Kingdom of our Lord and his Anointed.
He shall reign for ever and ever.
The twenty-four Elders, seated on their thrones before God,
Fell on their faces and worshipped God, saying,
"We thank you, O Lord, God almighty –
The One who is, the One who was –
Because you have asserted your great power and now reign.
The nations were angry, but now your wrath has come:
The time for the dead to be judged;
For the rewarding of your servants and prophets,
The Holy Ones and those in awe of your name,
Both small and great. **The time has come**
To destroy those who have destroyed the earth.
The temple of God in heaven is revealed;
So that the ark of his Covenant[1] was seen in his Temple.
There were bolts of lightning, rumblings of thunder,
An earthquake and a great hailstorm.

12 The birth of the Child. The Dragon is hurled to the ground with his angels

A great sign was seen in heaven –
A woman clothed with the sun and moon under her feet.
On her head a crown of twelve stars.
She was bearing a child.
Suffering the pangs of labour, she cried out in her distress
As she was about to give birth.

---

[1] The Ark of the Covenant was placed in the inner sanctum, the holy of holies, in the Temple, where only the High Priest was allowed to enter. In the Kingdom of Heaven, the inner sanctum would be open to all the Holy Ones.

Another sign was seen in heaven –
An enormous red Dragon,[1]
With seven heads and ten horns and seven crowns on its
    heads.
Its tails sweeps away a third of the stars of heaven and hurls
    them to the earth.

The Dragon stood in front of the woman about to give birth,
To devour her child as soon as it was born.[2]
She bore a male child, a son to shepherd all the nations with
    an iron staff.
Her child was snatched up to God to his Throne;
The woman fled into the desert to a place prepared for her by
    God to be looked after
For one thousand two hundred and sixty days.[3]

There was a battle in heaven:
Michael[4] and his angels fought with the dragon.
The Dragon and his angels fought back but did not prevail.
There was to be no longer any place for them in heaven.
The great Dragon – the first serpent,
Known as the Devil or Satan,[5] who misleads the whole world,
Was hurled down to the earth together with his angels.

I heard a loud voice in heaven say,
"The power of salvation has come –
The Kingdom of our God and the authority of his Anointed,
Because the prosecutor[6] of our brothers,

[1] This could be the Beast referred to earlier, see p. 127, fn. 1.
[2] The Devil is intent on devouring Christ. The drama of the life of Jesus on earth is preceded in heaven.
[3] Forty-two months. See p. 122, fn. 4.
[4] Michael is the archangel who is the guardian of Israel.
[5] It is interesting that in this instance, John explains the allegory. Could one infer that, when he does not, there is no reason for us to look for any, but just to enjoy the story?
[6] The word 'satan' means adversary or prosecutor in Hebrew. This was Satan's role in heaven, to question the righteousness of God's favourites, as is his role in the story of Job.

Who prosecutes them day and night before our God, has been
    cast down.
They overwhelmed him by the blood of the Lamb,[1]
And by the word of their testimony **to him.**
They did not love their lives so much as not to die **for him.**
Be glad O you heavens and you who live in them.
Woe to the earth and the sea because the Devil has gone down
To you with exceeding anger for he knows how brief is his time.

When the Dragon saw that he had been hurled to the earth,
He pursued the woman who bore the male child.[2]
The woman was given two wings of a great eagle
To fly to the place in the desert where she was looked after
For a period, periods and a half a period[3] out of the Serpent's[4]
    reach.
The Serpent spewed from his mouth water like a river
To overtake the woman and sweep her away in a torrent.
The earth assisted the woman by opening its mouth and
Swallowed the river that the Dragon had spewed from its
    mouth.
The Dragon went into a rage over the woman, and went off
To make war against the rest of her children –
Those who keep God's commandments,
And give testimony to **the divine nature of** Jesus.
I stood on the sand of the seashore.

[1] The fall of Satan from heaven is attributed to Jesus. Is this the primordial
prelude to the removal of Satan from earthly life by belief in the resurrected
Christ?
[2] The story line is: the dragon sought to devour the child on birth. When he
was snatched to safety in heaven, he returned there to find him. Michael
defeats him and he is thrown out of heaven. On earth, he seeks revenge on the
child's mother. If you were to ask, "Why was she not given a safe haven in
heaven?" the answer must be that we would not have such a good story.
[3] Literally, 'time'. 'Periods' means two periods. This phrase: 'time, times and
half a time' is taken from *Daniel* 7:25. There the reference is to the time that
Israel will suffer under the oppression of the wicked kingdom. With the
assumption that a period is 12 months, 3 periods would equal the previously
mentioned 42 months or 1,260 days. John is keeping us on our toes.
[4] The Dragon is now referred to as the Serpent.

13 The Beast from the sea with ten horns and seven heads

I saw a Beast[1] coming out of the sea with ten horns
And seven heads; on its horns were ten crowns.
On each of its heads were names of blasphemy.[2]
The Beast I saw looked like a leopard;
But its feet were like a bear's and its mouth like a lion's.
The Dragon gave the beast its power, its throne and great
    authority.
One of it heads appeared to have a fatal wound that had been
    healed.[3]
The whole world was mesmerised and followed the Beast.
They worshipped the Dragon because of the authority he had
    given to the Beast.[4]
They also worshipped the Beast and proclaimed,
"Who is as great as the Beast;
Who can make war against it?"
It was given a mouth to utter boasts and blasphemies.
It too was given the authority to rule for forty-two months.
It opened its mouth to utter blasphemies against God –
To blaspheme his name and dwelling place.
It was given the power to wage war against the Holy Ones,
And to overcome them; it was given control over every tribe
    and people, tongue and nation.

---

[1] The Dragon, Satan, designates the Beast to rule the world; like the Dragon he has seven heads and ten horns, but the Dragon had crowns on its heads rather than on its horns. As the horn represents strength, the ten horns could represent ten kingdoms or empires. In *Daniel*, there are four beasts that come out of the sea, who represent 'four kingdoms'; the fourth beast has ten horns, see p. 110, fn. 3.

[2] The names of pagan gods.

[3] The Dragon and the Beast seem to be the satanic counterparts "to Him who sits on the Throne" and to the Lamb. Like the Lamb, the Beast is fatally wounded but recovers. This is an indication that while earthly powers can be punished by God, through the intercession of Satan they can be restored to authority.

[4] This is an indication that while earthly powers can be punished by God, through the intercession of Satan, they can be restored to authority.

All the inhabitants on earth would worship him –
All whose names had not been recorded in the Book of Life[1]
Of the Lamb that was slain from the creation of the world.[2]

Let him who has an ear hear:
He who is destined for captivity will go into captivity.
He who is destined to fall by the sword will fall by the sword.
This is **test of** endurance and faith of the Holy Ones.

A second Beast whose name is 666

I saw another Beast coming out of the earth.[3]
It had two horns like a lamb but spoke like a Dragon;
It exercised all the power of the first Beast as its deputy.
It made all the inhabitants of earth worship the first Beast,
Whose fatal wound had been healed.
It performed great signs, making fire come down from
Heaven to earth in the sight of men.

Because of the signs he was able to perform on behalf of the
   first Beast,
It incited the inhabitants of the earth to make an image
To the Beast who, while struck by the sword, lived again.
It was given the power to give life to the image of the **first**
   Beast,
So that it could speak and order all those who did not worship
   it to be killed.
He also compelled everyone: small and great,
The rich and the poor, freemen and slaves

---

[1] These are those who did not believe in Christ.

[2] This is Pauline doctrine: The death of Christ was determined when the world
was created. It was the mystery to be revealed. See *Romans* 16:25; 1
Corinthians 2:7 and especially *Ephesians* 3:9–11.

[3] From what follows it would appear that it represents the false prophet who
can trick people to worship their earthly rulers rather than God and his Son. It
is even capable of performing miracles. But, if this is so, what is the use of the
faith in Jesus which is the result of his miracles?

To have a mark on his right hand or forehead[1],
So that no one could buy or sell without that mark –
The name of the Beast, or the name's numerical value.
This requires wisdom: let him with insight calculate from the
    number the name of the Beast;
For the number is of a man's name.
Its number is 666.[2]

14 The Lamb stands on Mount Zion

I looked and saw:
The Lamb was standing there on Mount Zion,[3]
With him were the hundred and forty four thousand men
With his and his father's name written on their foreheads.[4]
I heard a sound coming out of heaven like a torrent of waters
    and like great peals of thunder;
The sound I heard was also like that of harpists strumming
    their harps.
They sang a new song before the Throne and before the four
    Living Creatures and the Elders.
No one could learn the song except the hundred and forty-four
    thousand who had been ransomed from the earth.
These are those who had not defiled themselves with women[5],
    because they were chaste.
They follow the Lamb wherever he goes.

[1] The servants of God are given a protective seal against destruction in 7:3.
[2] In Hebrew, Greek and Latin, letters had a numerical value. There have been
many attempts to work out the conundrum of 666. None has been sufficiently
persuasive to achieve universal assent. The Hebrew spelling of Nero, *Neron
Caesar*, adds up to 666. As Nero was the first of the Emperors to persecute the
Christians, this is plausible. A popular commentary is that as 7 is the perfect
number, 6 is the imperfect number; hence 666 reflects the trebling of
imperfection.
[3] The site of the Temple.
[4] They are the ones who were given the protective seals in 7:3. Now we are
told that the seal was the names of God the Father and Christ.
[5] Sexual relations led to ritual impurity. The Israelites were forbidden to touch
women before they received the Ten Commandments at Mount Sinai.

They were ransomed from humankind as first fruits to God and
   to the Lamb.[1]
No lie is found in their mouth; they are without fault.

The first Angel of eternal good tidings

I saw another Angel flying in mid-air assigned to proclaim
   eternal good tidings to those who live on earth –
To every nation, tribe, tongue and people –
To declare in a loud voice: "Fear God and give him glory, for
   the hour of his judgement has come.
Worship him, who made heaven and earth, and the sea and
   the fountains of waters."

The second Angel declares the fall of Babylon

A second Angel followed and declared,
"Fallen! Fallen is Babylon[2]the great, that made all nations
Drink the wine of **God's** anger for her adulteries."[3]

The third Angel warns the worshippers of the Beast

A third Angel followed them and declared in a loud voice,
"Anyone who worships the Beast[4] and its image and receives
A mark on his forehead or his hand shall drink the wine of

---

[1] There is an irony here: according to Mosaic Law, the first-born belong to God.
Five *shekels* had to be given to the priesthood to redeem them from Temple
service; here God needs to redeem his servants from worldly powers, perhaps,
through the death of Jesus.

[2] These are the very words of Isaiah (21:9)

[3] Jeremiah (Ch.51) prophesies against Babylon for turning the whole world to
madness through drinking her wine. She had the opportunity to be forgiven
but did not take it; she will be severely punished. Babylon, as the evil ungodly
conqueror of Israel is the symbol of worldly power, in this instance Rome. Her
adulteries reveal her licentious unfaithfulness.

[4] The distinction between the sinners of 'Babylon' and worshippers of the Beast
may be that the former were those who were simply wicked while the latter
used religion as the basis for their wickedness.

God's fury, which has been poured undiluted into the cup of
    his wrath.
He will be tormented with burning sulphur in the presence of
    the Holy Angels and the Lamb.
And the smoke of their torment will rise for ever and ever.
There will be no rest day or night for those who worship the
    Beast and its image,
Or anyone who accepts the mark of its name."

[Now is the time for endurance from the Holy Ones –
Those who keep God's commandments and the faith in Jesus.
I heard a voice from heaven, "Write: Blessed are the dead –
Those who die in the Lord from now on."
"Yes," says the **Divine** Spirit, "they will rest from their
labour for their deeds will follow them."[1]]

The Man on the white cloud

I looked and saw: A white cloud, and seated on the cloud –
One 'like a son of man'[2] with a golden crown on his head and
    a sharp sickle in his hand.
Another Angel came out of the Temple[3] and called out in a
    loud voice to the one seated on the cloud,
"Take your sickle and reap,
Because the time to reap has come
For the harvest of the earth is ripe."
He who was seated on the cloud swung his sickle over the
    earth and the earth was harvested.

---

[1] They will in the future enjoy the rewards for their martyrdom. This
paragraph seems to a plea for patience from the faithful during their
persecution until the day of judgement.
[2] This is almost verbatim from *Daniel 7:13*. Often, ' like the son of man' is
perceived as Jesus; on other occasions, the perception is that of someone
looking like a man. I would think that Jesus is intended but, as he is almost
always referred to as the Lamb, I will allow my translation to reflect neutrality.
[3] The reader should remember that the latest vision is of the Lamb standing on
Mount Zion, the site of the Temple.

Another Angel came out of the Temple in heaven.[1]
He also had a sharp sickle;
Still another Angel in charge of the fire, left the altar
And called in a loud voice to him with the sharp sickle,
"Thrust your sharp sickle and gather the clusters from the
grapes from the earth's vine because its grapes are ripe."
The Angel swung his sickle on the earth and gathered its
grapes
And threw them into the winepress of God's great wrath.[2]
They were trampled in the winepress outside the city.
Blood flowed out of the press, rising as high as horses' bridles
for a distance of 1,600 furlongs.[3]

15 The seven Angels bearing seven plagues sing a new song to God and the Lamb

I saw another sign in heaven – great and wonderful:
Seven Angels with the last seven plagues, with which to bring
to an end God's anger.[4]
I saw what appeared as a sea of glass blazing with fire;
I also saw standing on the glassy sea those who had
vanquished the Beast and its image and
those with the number of its name on them.
They held harps of God and were singing the song of Moses
and the song of the Lamb:[5]
"Great and wonderful are your works, Lord God Almighty;

---

[1] It would appear that Mount Zion and its Temple had a counterpart in heaven.

[2] The grapes are those who worship the Beast; their blood, not wine, comes out of the winepress.

[3] That is about 200 miles.

[4] The reader will recall the previous seven Angels who sounded their trumpets to signal destruction for the wicked. The narrator appears to be suggesting that the previous three angels were bearing plagues. This would be like the ten plagues with which God afflicted Egypt, the first of the worldly empires, which rejected the Jewish God.

[5] In the previous chapter we read of the 144,000, with harps, singing a new song to the Lamb, see p. 129.

Righteous and true are your ways, King of all nations;
Who shall not fear you, O Lord, and glorify your name?
Because you alone are holy, all the nations will come
And worship before you for your judgements have been
   vindicated."[1]
After this, I saw the Tabernacle of the Testimony revealed in
   heaven.
The seven Angels bearing the seven plagues came out of the
   Temple.
They were dressed in pure white linen and wore golden sashes
   around their chests.
One of the four Living Creatures gave to the seven Angels
   seven golden bowls, filled with the wrath of God,
Who lives for ever and ever.
And the heavens were filled with smoke,
The emanation of God's glory and might –
No one could enter God's Temple until
The seven plagues of the seven Angels had been fulfilled

16 The seven plagues from the seven bowls

I heard a loud voice from the Temple tell the seven Angels,
"Go, pour out the seven bowls of God's anger on earth!"
The first went and poured out his bowl on the earth,
And ugly and painful sores broke out on the men who had
The mark of the Beast and who worshipped its image.

The second Angel went and poured out his bowl into the sea:
It turned into blood like that of a dead man;
Every creature that lived in the sea died.

The third Angel poured out his bowl into the rivers and water
   springs:
They too turned into blood.

---

[1] The song of Moses, *Exodus* 15:11: 'Who is like you, among the gods, O LORD;
who is like you, glorious in divinity?' (My translation)

I heard the Angel of the waters say,
"You are righteous, you who are and were because of this –
   your judgement.
As they have shed the blood of Holy Ones and Prophets,
It is right that you have given them blood to drink."
I heard the Altar respond:
"Yes, Lord God Almighty, your judgements are true and just."

The fourth Angel poured out his bowl on the sun:
So, it was given the power to scorch men with fire.
Seared by the great heat, they cursed the name of the God
Who ordained these plagues and did not repent.
So as not to give him glory.

The fifth poured out his bowl on the throne of the Beast:
Its kingdom was plunged into darkness;
They gnawed their tongues because of their pain.
They blasphemed the God of heaven
Because of their pains and sores but did not repent of their
   works.

The sixth poured out his bowl into the great Euphrates
   River:
Its water dried up to prepare a highway for the kings of the
   East.[1]

Interlude before the seventh plague: The three demonic spirits

I saw, coming out of the mouth of the
Dragon and out of the mouth of the Beast
And out of the mouth of the False Prophet,[2]
Three defiled spirits looking like frogs.

[1] This is a highway for their journey into perdition.
[2] It is a good time to recall that the Dragon is symbolic of Satan, the fallen angel, the Beast, his human deputy, most likely the Roman Emperor who was persecuting the Christians, and the False Prophet, the pagan priests who justified their master's behaviour.

They are the demonic spirits performing signs;
They go to the kings of the earth,
To assemble them for battle
On the great day of the Almighty God.[1]

Behold, I come like a thief![2]
Blessed is the one on guard, clothed, so that he may not be
  found naked and men see his shame.
They assembled the kings in the place, known in Hebrew as
  Armageddon.[3]

The seventh plague

The seventh Angel poured out his bowl in the air:
A loud voice was heard from the Throne in the Temple saying,
"It has been done!" There were bolts of lightning,
Rumbling noises, peals of thunder and a great earthquake,
The earthquake was so great – there had been nothing like it
  since when Man was on earth.
The great city[4] was split into three parts and
The cities of the nations fell into ruin.
The sins of great Babylon[5] were remembered before God

[1] This is the Day of Judgement.
[2] This is God, Jesus or his representative who is speaking. It is a favourite
image of the gospels: redemption will appear when it is not expected, even in
the midst of great persecution, when the forces of evil are arrayed in great
power.
[3] Literally: *Har Meggido*, Mount Megiddo, the place where the righteous,
reforming King Josiah was slain by Pharoah-necho, the king of Egypt, in 608
BCE. It will now become the scene where the empires of the earth will suffer
destruction.
[4] Babylon.
[5] According to biblical tradition, Babylon was the place where a united
humanity sought to scale the heavens by building a great ziggurat. To
confound them God confused their languages to prevent them from
communicating with each other. As the first city to challenge God and the
place of many languages, there could be no better symbol for the arrogance of
human power. The identification of Rome with Babylon is confirmed later, see
p. 137. As capital of the Empire; it was both the chief tormentor of Christians
and a multi-lingual city.

To give her the cup of the wine of his furious wrath.
Every island fled; mountains disappeared from sight.
Great hailstones, each a talent in weight, fell on men;
They cursed God because of the hail,
Because of the great severity of the plague

17 The Crimes of Babylon

One of the seven Angels with the seven bowls said to me,
"Come, I will show you the judgement of
The great whore who sits on many waters.[1]
The kings of the earth committed adultery with her;[2]
The inhabitants of the earth became drunk with the wine of
her adulteries."[3]

In my vision[4], he then carried me away into the wilderness.
I saw a woman sitting on a Scarlet Beast covered with names
of blasphemy.
It had seven heads and ten horns.[5]
The Woman was dressed in purple and scarlet,
Decked in gold, jewels and pearls;
She had a gold cup in her hand, filled with abominations and
The filth of her adulteries.

On her forehead was written a cryptic name:

BABYLON THE GREAT
THE MOTHER OF WHORES
AND THE
ABOMINATIONS OF THE EARTH

---

[1] Rome, like Babylon and all great cities are situated on rivers
[2] New alliances are made which break old treaties. Diplomacy was based on treachery, deceit and unfaithfulness – the pernicious aspects of adultery.
[3] All who live in their countries are swept up in the corruption of their rulers.
[4] Literally: in the spirit.
[5] The Beast that came out of the sea (p. 127) also had seven heads and ten horns. It could be the same beast or another in the narrator's vision.

I saw that the woman was drunk from the blood of the
Holy Ones and the blood of the witnesses to Jesus.
I was totally mystified by the sight of her.
The Angel asked me, "Why are you so mystified?[1]
I will explain the mystery of the Woman and the Beast
With seven heads and ten horns carrying her.
The Beast that you saw lived, died,[2] but will arise from the
    abyss to go to its **final** destruction:
The inhabitants of earth, whose names have not been recorded
    in the Book of Life since the creation of the world[3]
Will be amazed when they see the Beast,
When they see the Beast who lived, died and lives[4] **again.**"

The Whore of Babylon is Rome

"This requires an understanding mind:
The seven heads are the seven hills[5] on which the Woman sits.
They are also seven kings[6]: five are fallen, one is, and one is
    yet to come.
When he comes, he will rule for a short time.

---

[1] This question only makes sense because it is the sole time that the narrator
expresses his astonishment at the extraordinary sights he has seen in his vision.
[2] Literally: 'was and is not'. The earthly powers suffered defeat when Jesus,
through his death, triumphed over them. They have been restored to life by
Satan but will meet their final and absolute defeat at Armaggedon.
[3] As noted in a previous footnote, this is part of Pauline theology: the drama of
Christ was preordained; so too were those individuals to be condemned and to
be saved. This would be a contradiction of free will except if one sees that the
mind of God is timeless, so that there are no distinctions between past, present
and future. St. Paul believed, that at the birth of the sinning Adam, the
antidote, Christ, the man-god was also created: "Before the foundations of the
earth were established he chose us through Christ . . .he predestined us to
become his adopted sons through Jesus Christ. (*Ephesians*: 1:4,5)
[4] Literally: 'is present'.
[5] This is proof positive that Babylon is the symbol of Rome, as she was the city
known by all to have been built on seven hills.
[6] These are likely to be representative of great kingdoms. The five that are
described as fallen would be Egypt, Assyria, Babylon, Persia and Greece. The
sixth would be Rome. The one to come could be at the time when the
'Barbarians' were dividing the Roman Empire.

The Beast who once lived and once died is an eighth king –
Who encompasses the seven – is heading for destruction.
The ten horns that you saw are ten kings[1] who have not yet
    been enthroned,
But have been given the power of kings for a short period
    along with the Beast.
These are of one mind; they will give their power and be
    subordinate to the Beast."

"They will make war against the Lamb,
But the Lamb will overcome them because
He is the Lord of lords and the King of kings –
With him will be those he called the chosen and faithful."

The Angel said : "The waters you saw where the whore sits,
Are the peoples, the multitude of nations and tongues.[2]
The ten horns you saw and the Beast will hate the whore;
They will bring her to ruin, strip her naked, eat her flesh and
    consume her in fire.
For God has inspired them to accomplish his desire –
To unite them in giving to the Beast their power to rule,
Until the words of God are fulfilled.
The Woman you saw is the great city that rules over the kings
    of the earth."[3]

18 The Fall of Babylon

After this, I saw another Angel with great authority
Descending from heaven; the earth was lit up by his glory.
He cried out with a mighty voice,
"Fallen, fallen is Babylon the Great.
She has become the home for demons,

---

[1] These could refer to the chieftains of the 'barbarian tribes' who were
successfully rebelling against Rome.

[2] As the sea is tempestuous, so are the nations of the world.

[3] The destruction of Rome by the ten barbarian kings will be part of the process
for the achievement of the victory of the Lamb.

The cage for every defiled spirit,
The cage for every defiled and detestable bird.
Because all the nations have drunk the wine of wrath[1]
    of her adulteries.
The kings of the earth committed adultery with her.
The earth's merchants became rich from her love of luxury."

I heard another voice from heaven say,
"Leave her, my people, lest you share in her sins;
Lest you receive her plagues – her sins pile up to heaven.
God has remembered her crimes.
Pay her back in her own coin
Repay her double for what she has done.
In the cup she mixed, mix her a double dose.
In proportion to her self-indulgence and luxuries,
Give her as much torment and grief."

"In her heart, she says,
'I rule as queen;
I am not a widow,
I will experience no mourning.'
Therefore, in one day, plagues will strike her:
Death and mourning and famine.
She will be consumed by fire,
For mighty is the Lord God who judges her."

"When the kings of the earth, who committed adultery with
    her
And shared her luxuries see the smoke from her burning,
They will weep and mourn over her.
Standing far off, because they are terrified by her torment,
They will exclaim,
'Woe, woe O great city;
Babylon, O powerful city,
In one hour, your judgement has arrived.'

---

[1] That is God's wrath.

The earth's merchants weep and mourn over her
Because no one buys their cargoes of gold, silver, jewels,
Pearls, fine linen, silk, purple and scarlet cloth,
All sorts of fragrant woods, all articles of ivory,
Costly wood, bronze, iron and marble,
Cinnamon and spice, incense, myrrh and frankincense,
Wine and oil, fine meal and cereals, cattle and sheep,
Horses and carriages; and the bodies and souls of men."

"They will say,
'The fruit your soul lusted after has vanished from you.
All your treasured and colourful things have disappeared,
Never to be found again.'
The merchants who were enriched by selling these things
Will stand far off, terrified at her torment.
They will weep, mourn and cry out,
'Woe, woe, O great city,
Dressed in fine linen, purple and scarlet,
Decked in gold, jewels and pearls.
In an hour, such great wealth has been laid waste.' "

"Every sea master, every seafarer, sailor, all who earn their
    living from the sea, will stand far off.
When they see the smoke from her burning, they will exclaim,
'Was there anything like this great city?'
They will throw dust on their heads; weeping and mourning,
They will cry out,
'Woe! Woe! O great city!
All who had ships in the sea became rich through her.
In an hour, she has been laid waste.'
Rejoice over her, O heaven, Holy Ones, Apostles and Prophets!
For God has judged her for condemning you."

A mighty Angel lifted a rock, the size of a large millstone
And hurled it into the sea and said,
"With such tumult, the great city Babylon will be cast down,
Never to be restored again.

The sound of harpists, musicians, flutists and trumpeters will
    never be heard in you again.
No craftsman of any skill will ever be found in you again.
The sound of a millstone will never be heard in you again.
The light of a lamp shall never shine in you again.
The voice of a bridegroom and bride will never be heard in you
    again.
Your merchants were the world's important men.
By your sorcery, were all the nations deceived.
In her were found the blood of the Prophets and Holy Ones
And all **good men** who have been killed on the earth.

19 The Glorification of God

After this, I heard a noise like a great crowd shouting in
    heaven:
"Halleluyah![1]
Salvation, glory and power is our God's,
For his judgements are true and righteous
He has judged the great Whore
Who defiled the earth by her adulteries.
He avenged the blood of his servants by her hand."
Again they shouted,
"Halleluyah!
The smoke from her rises for ever and ever."
The twenty-four Elders and the four Living Creatures
Fell down and worshipped God, who was seated on the Throne.
They cried: "Amen! Halleluyah!"
Then a voice was heard from the Throne,
"Praise our God, all you, his servants,
You who fear him, both small and great."

---

[1] The word is the transliteration of the Hebrew, *hallelu Yah*, meaning: Praise
Yah (the abbreviated form of Yahweh).

The Wedding of the Lamb

Then I heard a noise like of a great crowd,
Like the roar of many rushing waters,
Like crashing peals of thunder, shouting,
"Halleluyah!
For our Lord God Almighty reigns,
Let us rejoice and exult; we will render him glory;
For the wedding of the Lamb has come,
And his Bride[1] has prepared herself:
Fine linen – bright and clean, for the fine linen is
The righteous deeds of the Holy Ones."[2]

Then the Angel instructed me, "Write:
'Blessed are those who have been summoned to
the wedding supper of the Lamb.'"
He also said, "These are the true words of God."
I fell at his feet to worship him. He said **in protest** to me,
"Do you not see that I am a fellow-servant with you and
With your brothers who believe in the testimony to Jesus?[3]
Worship God!
Those testifying to Jesus have the spirit of prophecy."

The Man on the white horse

I saw the heavens open up and there before me was a white
    horse,[4]
The one seated on it is named "Faithful and True".
With righteousness, he renders judgement and goes to war.
His eyes were like blazing fire;

---

[1] The bride is the community of Holy Ones – the Church of Christ.
[2] It is interesting that, when the narrator wishes to explain his symbolism, he does so.
[3] That he was the Son of God and the sacrificial lamb to redeem the world from sin and death.
[4] When the Lamb opened the first seal, a white horse appeared, whose rider, wearing a crown, sets forth to conquer the world (6:2). What follows suggests that it is the same white horse.

On his head were many diadems.
A name is written on him that only he understands.
He is dressed in a robe dipped in blood.
The name that has been given to him is "The Word of God".[1]
The armies of heaven followed him on white horses,
Dressed in white linen – white and clean.[2]

From his mouth emerges a sharp sword to smite the nations;
He will shepherd them with an iron staff.
He will tread the winepress of the fury of the wrath of God
    Almighty.
On his robe and on his thigh, his name has been written:
KING OF KINGS AND LORD OF LORDS.

I saw one Angel standing in the sun.
He cried out in a loud voice to the birds flying in mid-air:
"Come, assemble yourselves for the great feast of God –
So that you may eat the flesh of kings, commanders, heroes,
Of horses and their riders, the flesh of all men –
Freemen and slaves, the commoner and the nobleman."

Then I saw the Beast, the kings of the earth – their armies,
Assembled to make war against him who rode the horse and
    his army.
The Beast was captured, and along with him the False Prophet,
Who had performed signs for it, by which he had deceived
Those who had received the mark of the Beast and had
    worshipped his image.
The two[3] were thrown alive into the fiery lake of burning sulphur.

---

[1] This would indicate that he is Christ as his robe is dipped in blood and he is
the Word –Christ was at the beginning of the world and the purpose of
creation was for man to find fulfilment through Christ. This is the nub of
Pauline theology developed in the Gospel according to St. John.
[2] As we were just told that the Bride of the Lamb was dressed in fine linen,
bright and clean, and this represented the righteous deeds of the Holy Ones, it
is right to conclude that the heavenly army includes those who gave testimony
to Christ.
[3] The Beast and the False Prophet.

The rest were killed by the sword that emerged from
The mouth of him who was seated on the horse and
All the birds gorged themselves on their flesh.[1]

20 Satan is imprisoned for a thousand years, the First Resurrection

I saw an Angel descending from heaven with the key to
The Abyss and a large chain in his hand.
He laid hold of the Dragon, the Ancient Serpent who is the
Devil and Satan, and bound him for a thousand years.
He hurled him into the Abyss, closed and sealed it over
   him,
So that he should no longer deceive the nations
Until the completion of the thousand years.
Then, he would be released for a little while.

I saw thrones;
Seated on them were those given the power to judge.
I saw the souls of those who had been beheaded because of
Their testimony for Jesus and because of the word of God.[2]
They had not worshipped the Beast or its image;
Nor did they receive its mark on their foreheads or hands.
They came to life and reigned with Christ a thousand years,
While the rest of the dead[3] did not come to life again until the
   completion of the thousand years.
This is the first resurrection.
Blessed and holy is the one is the one who partakes in the first
   resurrection.

---

[1] Significantly, Christ alone is responsible for the victory against the Beast; also the birds feeding on the flesh of the enemies is inspired by the description of the apocalypse in *Ezekiel*, chs.38 and 39.

[2] Does 'because of the word of God' imply that their deaths were preordained to entitle them to the blessing of sitting on thrones next to Christ?

[3] The rest of the dead could be believers who had not suffered martyrdom or persecution, or perhaps even the righteous who lived before Christ or had not known Christ but had lived spiritual non-worldly lives.

The second death[1] has no power over them.
But, they will be priests to God and Christ
And will reign with him for a thousand years.

The last battle against Satan and The Day of Judgement

When these thousand years are completed,
Satan will be released from prison and will set out to
deceive the nations in the four corners of the earth –
Gog and Magog,[2] to muster them for the war,
Whose numbers were as the sand of the sea.
They marched across the breadth of the land and
Surrounded the camp of the Holy Ones and the beloved city.[3]
But fire from heaven consumed them.
The Devil who had deceived them was hurled into a lake of

---

[1] The 'second death' is a mystery. For me, its meaning can be found in St.
Paul's belief that at the 'second coming'/ the day of judgement (which he
believed would come in his own lifetime), the living faithful witnesses to Christ
would join the dead witnesses in the heavenly clouds. According to St. Paul,
those who were baptised in Christ had, through his death and resurrection,
died to sin and had gained eternal life. In his letter to the Thessalonians, 4:
13–18, he writes of this faith: 'The dead in Christ will be the first to rise. Then
we who are still alive will be caught up together with them into the clouds to
meet the Lord in the air. This is the way we shall be with the Lord forever
(4:16,17) – the 'first resurrection'. John the Divine is therefore confirming that
those who 'died' in Christ while alive would not have to suffer a second
(physical) death. *St. John* agrees – see 5:24;8:51.

[2] Gog is the archetype of evil for Ezekiel. In his prophecy of the apocalyptic
battle, Gog lives in a place called Magog: 'Son of man, look towards Gog, the
land of Magog, the chief prince of Meshech and Tubal and prophesy against
him.' (38:2) Meshech and Tubal are listed as two of the sons of Japheth
(*Genesis* 10:2) who was one of the three sons of Noah. The son not mentioned
is Jaban, the ancestor of the Ionians. The geographical site of Magog is a
source of speculation. Ezekiel refers to the three brothers as traders in slaves
and brass (27:13). In view of the text's condemnation of worldly affairs, this
may be significant in the choice of Gog as an arch-villain. What is also of
interest is that in rabbinic literature, Gog and Magog are identified, as in this
text, as the assembly of wicked nations. The numerical value of the Hebrew
letters of 'Gog and Magog' add up to 70, the ancient supposed number of the
nations of the world.

[3] Jerusalem.

burning sulphur, where the Beast and False Prophet are.
They will be tormented day and night throughout the
 ages.

I saw a great white Throne and Him who was seated on it.
Earth and heaven fled from his presence –
No place was found for them.[1]
I saw the dead, commoners and noblemen standing before the
 Throne.
The books **of Judgement** were opened;
Another book was opened – the Book of Life.
The dead were judged in accordance to what was recorded in
 them about their actions.[2]

The sea surrendered its dead and they were judged according
 to their works.
Death and Hades were hurled into the lake of fire.[3]
This is the second death[4] – the lake of fire!
Anyone whose name was not found in the Book of Life –
He was cast into the lake of fire.[5]

21 A New Heaven and a New Earth

Then I saw a new heaven and a new earth,
For the first earth and the first heaven had passed away and
 the sea was no longer there.[6]

---

[1] The end of the earth and sky suggests the end of the physical world. See later in 21:1.

[2] It is significant that no mention is made about their faith or lack of it.

[3] Even death and the shadowy underworld of Hades come to an end.

[4] This is not the same 'second death' as referred to earlier, for there would be no possibility of witnesses to Jesus being thrown into the fiery lake of hell.

[5] We are given a confused picture of the fate of the wicked. While we are told previously that those who were not in the Book of Life, but in the other books, were judged according to their deeds, here we are told that all of them were thrown into the fiery lake. There seem to be no degrees of distinction between the un-saved in regard to their awful punishment.

[6] This is the undoing of the world's creation. Life ends on earth and only the blessed live with God and his Son and the heavenly hosts of Angels.

I saw the Holy City, the New Jerusalem, descending from
    heaven from God,
Prepared as a bride, beautifully adorned for her husband.

I heard a loud voice from the Throne saying,
"Now the Tabernacle[1] of God is with men;
He will dwell with them and they will be his peoples
And God, himself, will be with them.
He will wipe every tear from their eyes.
There will be no more death,
Nor mourning, nor wailing, nor pain
For the first order of things has passed away."[2]

He who was seated on the Throne said,
"See, I am making all things new."
He says, "Write, for these words are reliable and true."
Again, he says to me, "It is accomplished!
I am the Alpha and the Omega, the Beginning and the End.
To him who is thirsty, I will freely give to drink from
The fountain of the waters of life.
He who is victorious will inherit all of this.
I will be God to him and he will be to me a son.[3]
But, the cowardly and faithless, the depraved and murderers,
The fornicators and sorcerers, the idolaters and deceivers of all
    sorts –
Their fate is the fiery lake of burning sulphur.
This is the second death."

The Heavenly Jerusalem

One of the seven Angels who had the seven bowls with the
    seven final plagues came to me and said,

---

[1] This is God's dwelling.
[2] Sadly, as the visionary cannot imagine or cope with the natural world
because there can be no absence of pain, he longs for eternal paradise, even
though it means the end of the earth.
[3] He will be like Jesus.

"Come, I will show you the Bride, the wife of the Lamb."
He carried me away in spirit to a great and high mountain,[1]
And showed me the Holy City, Jerusalem,[2]
Descending from heaven from God.
It was suffused with the glory of God.
Its brilliance was like that of a very precious jewel – like jasper,
    clear as crystal.
It had a great and high wall with twelve gates.
At the gates were twelve Angels; over them were inscribed the
    names of the twelve tribes of Israel.
On the east were three gates; on the north – three gates;
On the south – three gates; on the west – three gates.
The wall of the City had twelve foundation stones.
Over them were the names of the twelve Apostles of the
    Lamb.

The Angel who was speaking to me had a gold measuring rod
    to measure the City, its gate and wall.[3]
The City was laid out as a square, equal in length and width.
He measured the City with a rod – twelve thousand furlongs –
The length, the width and height were equal.[4]
He measured its wall and it was a hundred and forty four
    cubits high,[5]by human measurements used by the Angel.
The wall was built of jasper and the City of pure gold.

[1] Ezekiel describes a similar experience: 'In the visions from God, he brought me into the land of Israel and set me down on a very high mountain . . .' (40:2). The prophet's vision of a new Jerusalem was the likely inspiration for John the Divine. The concluding verse of the book of *Ezekiel* tells us that the city will be renamed: *Yahweh Sha'ma* – Yahweh is There.

[2] In this instance, the New Jerusalem is the Bride of the Lamb.

[3] Ezekiel also sees a 'man whose appearance is like brass' measuring the city (40:3).

[4] This is a gargantuan size, especially for its height: 1,500 miles. Even if one assumes that the city was sited on the great and tall mountain, and its height included its measurement from the ground, it would still be spectacular! Also, how long would it have taken to do such a measurement? The lesson for readers is to realise that they are meant to be astonished. All will be possible at the end of days.

[5] About 200 feet.

The foundations of the City's wall were adorned with every
    kind of jewels.
The first foundation – jasper; the second – sapphire;
The third – agate; the fourth – emerald; the fifth – onyx;
The sixth – cornelian; the seventh – chrysolite;
The eighth – beryl; the ninth – topaz; the tenth – emerald;
The eleventh – jacinth; the twelfth – amethyst.
The twelve gates were twelve pearls –
Each gate was fashioned from a single pearl.
The City Street was pure gold, translucent as glass.

I saw no Temple in it for the Lord God Almighty and the Lamb
    are its Temple.
The City has no need for the sun or moon to shine on it
For the glory gives it light and the Lamb is its lamp.
And the nations shall walk by its light;
The kings will bring their splendour into it.[1]
Its gates will never close because it will not know night.
They will bring the glory and honour of the nations into it.
No profane thing will enter into it, or anyone who behaves
    abominably or deceitfully;
But only those listed in the Book of Life of the Lamb.

22 The Water and Tree of Life

The Angel showed me the River of the Water of Life,
As clear as crystal, flowing from the Throne of God and of the
    Lamb down the City Street.
On each side of the river was a Tree of Life bearing twelve
    crops of fruit, yielding its fruit every month.
The leaves of the Trees will be for the healing of nations.
There will be no more curses.

The Throne of the God and the Lamb will be in it;
And his servants will serve him; they will see his face;

[1] This is in fulfilment of the prophecy that all nations shall go to Jerusalem
(*Isaiah* 2:2,3)

And the name of God will be on their foreheads.[1]
There will be no more night.
They will have no need the light of a lamp or of the sun
Because the Lord God will shed light on them,
And they will reign for ever and ever.

John's vision will soon be realized

The Angel said to me, "These words are reliable and true;
The Lord, the God who inspired the Prophets, sent his Angel
To show his servants what would soon happen.
Realise that I will come quickly.
Blessed is he who takes to heart
The prophetic message of this book."

I, John, am the one who heard and saw these things.
When I had heard and seen them,
I fell in worship at the feet of the Angel,
Who had shown me these things. He protested,
"Do you not see that I am a fellow-servant with you
And your brothers, the prophets and those who take to heart
The words of this book. Worship God, **not me**!"

Then, he told me,
"Do not keep secret the prophetic message of this book because
the time is near.
Let the wicked continue in his wickedness;
Let the profane continue in their profanity;
Let the righteous continue in their righteousness and
Let the holy continue in their holiness!"[2]

---

[1] This is extraordinary as the name of God was ineffable, and now it is revealed on the foreheads of his servants.

[2] The Angel is telling John that, in spite of the wondrous destiny of the righteous and the horrific fate of the wicked at the end of the old world, it is not his responsibility to seek to make any changes in human behaviour; it is too late, for the end is approaching too rapidly.

Jesus speaks to John

"Behold, I am coming soon[1] and my reward is with me –
I will give to each man according to his works.
I am the Alpha and the Omega,
The First and the Last,
The Beginning and the End."[2]

"Blessed are those who wash their robes,[3]
So that they have the right to the Tree of Life,
And may enter the gates of the City.
Outside are the dogs,[4] the sorcerers, the fornicators,
The murderers, the isolators and everyone
Who loves and practises treachery.
I, Jesus, have sent my angel to you to give testimony
Of these things to the Churches.
I am the root and the offspring of David –[5]
The bright morning star."

John's admonition and warning

The **Divine** Spirit and the Bride[6] say, "Come!"
Let him who hears this also say, "Come!"

---

[1] The person speaking is no longer the angel but Jesus. The transformation of the angel into God is not uncommon in the Hebrew Bible. An angel is the agent – the manifestation of the godhead – and, therefore, can suddenly become God, himself. An example of this is the appearance to Moses of the angel in the burning bush, who suddenly becomes God, *Exodus*, chapter 3.

[2] This is further confirmation of the theology of St. Paul developed by St. John's gospel that Christ was created at the beginning of time, as the human/divine antidote to the sinful Adam. The idea that great souls were created before their realisation in the flesh was an ancient Rabbinic idea..

[3] Of course, the robes are symbolic of earthly behaviour. The chosen will gain the right to eat from the Tree of Life, and achieve eternity, the right removed from Adam because of his initial disobedience.

[4] Biblically, there can be nothing worse than being identified as a dog.

[5] As the Son of God, and his sacrificial Lamb for the redemption of the world, the relationship of Jesus to David seems irrelevant, but it is necessary for the Church to associate him with the Messianic hopes of the Jewish people, from whom Jesus sprung.

[6] The Bride is the community of Christ.

Whoever is thirsty let him come
And drink freely from the water of life.

I give warning to everyone who hears the prophetic words of
    this book:
If anyone adds to them, God will add to him
The plagues recorded in this book.
And if anyone takes away any words from this book,
God will take away from him his share in
The Tree of Life and in the Holy City,
Described in this book.

The Coming of Jesus

He who testified to these things says,
"Yes, I am coming soon!"

Amen. Come, Lord Jesus.

The grace of the Lord Jesus be with God's people. Amen